Creating
EMPTY BOTTLE MOMENTS

Creating
EMPTY BOTTLE MOMENTS
CLIVE BERKMAN

Jim,
From my kitchen
to yours -- SHALOM!!!
Wishing you days filled with empty
bottle moments.

Clive Berkman
October 2008.

Cooking
with
Clive

Cover photography by Scott Brignac and Cody Bess
Cover and jacket design by Scott Brignac
Interior layout and design by Anne McLaughlin, Blue Lake Design, Dickinson, Texas
Photography credits are found on page 254 and constitute an extension of this copyright page.

Published in the United States by Baxter Press, Friendswood, Texas
Printed in China

ISBN: 978-1-888237-71-9

To Ian, thanks for so many empty bottle memories ... and the ones to come.

Contents

PREFACE
Empty Bottles Tell the Best Stories

As I look back over my years in the restaurant business and cooking for my friends and family, a single theme surfaces again and again: empty bottles. For years, I've kept empty bottles that remind me of warm and wonderful times. Full bottles speak of possibilities, but empty ones tell great stories about couples celebrating an anniversary, parents enjoying a child's birthday, an engagement, a graduation, and a hundred other treasured moments. All the work of preparation, attention to detail, and presentation are designed to create those magic moments from the raw ingredients of food, creativity, and love. To me, empty bottles symbolize memorable moments in the richest relationships in life. And for that reason, they aren't empty at all—they're actually full and overflowing with meaning.

Every page of this book has reawakened wonderful memories for me. Each event, whether long ago in my childhood or just last week, reminds me of people who touched my life, and whose lives I hope I touched in some way. As I've been working on this book, I've reconnected with people who worked with me at Charley's 517, True Concessions, Crème de la Crème Catering, guests who dined at the restaurant, and students I taught at the University of Houston. Over the years, many of them encouraged me (many times) to write a cookbook, but they didn't want it to be "just a cookbook." They wanted me to tell the story of my life and the memories we shared—that's why this cookbook is different from most of those on your shelves. Several told me that they learned the best lessons of their lives during our time together. Their words—and the sincere look on their faces—mean the world to me, but whatever they learned from me pales in comparison to what I learned from them. Life in the restaurant business was an exhilarating, challenging, inspiring experience, and it set the stage for the most monumental transformation in my life.

In these pages, I want to communicate my philosophy of cooking and share the lessons I learned about cooking, about people, and about life from my time as a restaurant manager and chef. I didn't want to give you a long, tedious list of recipes (even really good ones). Instead, I wanted to take you on a journey back to the most significant dinners and recreate those moments for you. You'll read about the election night dinner for George Bush (#41), serving jerk chicken at a festival at a park in downtown Houston, a black tie dinner when our guests tasted 34 different vintages of a single chateau in the city's only underground cellar, serving ribeyes to Van Halen, and many other memorable events. For each one, you'll find the menu and recipes so you can create special moments for the people who mean the most to you. Since I live and work in Houston, most of the people and events described in this book are from here. The lessons, recipes, and tips, however, apply to people all across the country, and, in fact, around the world. Good cooking isn't provincial.

My philosophy of cooking and my philosophy of life combine two seemingly opposite traits: a commitment to excellence and a light-hearted joy. Some people become obsessive about doing everything perfectly, and they don't enjoy cooking, the presentation of the meal, or the people they serve. As you'll see in several places in this book, I believe there are more important things than getting everything perfect. If you make a mistake, don't worry about it. If you don't have exactly the right ingredients, use what you have and create a new dish. It may be even better than the original recipe! Develop some basic skills, and add a huge dollop of creativity and love to everything you do.

I hope you enjoy the recipes, but more than that, I hope you gain some insight and inspiration from the lessons I've learned about creating empty bottle moments. You'll find that a few small changes in the way you think about food, the way you prepare it, and the way you serve it can make your meals and your life richer than ever before. My philosophy consists of "recipes for life."

"What's a Nice Jewish Boy Like You Doing in the Kitchen?"

Since I was a small boy, I've loved everything about food. I enjoyed tasting things other boys my age wouldn't touch. I was fascinated as I watched my mother cook dinner, and the smells of her kitchen captivated me. As I grew up, I realized that it wasn't just the end product of cooking that interested me; the complexity and creativity of the process captured my imagination. The pressure to put something special on a plate wasn't a threat to me—it was a challenge I was thrilled to take on. But before I get ahead of myself, let me tell you a bit about my background. At each turning point in my life, people have asked, "What's a nice Jewish boy like you doing in the kitchen?" Here's my answer. . . .

The Engineer and the Actress

My parents met on the beach in mid-winter in Durban, South Africa. One day on holiday, my father took a photograph between the legs of some of his friends, and that night

Clockwise from top: My mother, Maureen, on her wedding day; at the beach in Durban, South Africa with my mother, 1959; my family, 1975; my paternal grandmother

he developed the image in a darkroom. As he looked at the picture, he noticed a strikingly pretty woman in the distance. He thought, *Who is that beautiful girl? I've got to meet her!* In those days, the beaches weren't crowded, especially in the winter, so it wasn't hard for him to find her the next day. He introduced himself, and as they talked, he became even more impressed with her. They began dating, and before long, they married. My parents were as different as night and day. My father was a straight-laced chemical engineer; my mother was an actress. Their relationship was like vinaigrette.

On their honeymoon, they went to Kruger National Park. The first night, my mother cooked a rump roast, which she burnt to a crisp. My father glared at it and pronounced, "Maureen, you'd better learn how to cook."

My mother took his criticism as a challenge, and she became one of the best cooks I've ever known. In fact, she became so accomplished that she started a catering business and taught cooking classes. As a little boy, I sat in the back and soaked up everything she taught those ladies. One of the reasons my mother poured herself into cooking is that my father insisted that she give up her acting career when they married. In that culture, women stayed at home and took care of their families.

I'm the oldest child in the family. Eight years after I was born, my brother Antony came along, and Patricia followed two years later.

My father's family emigrated from Germany; my mother's ancestry is Lithuanian. When we think of persecution of the Jews, we usually think of the Nazis and the Holocaust of World War II, but both sides of my family fled from persecution in Europe during the First World War.

My father's mother was one of the strongest, toughest women I've ever known. Every Sunday, she came to our house for dinner and an inspection. We were a fairly well-to-do family with several servants. When my grandmother walked in each week, the servants suddenly vanished because they were terrified of her. She put on a white glove and went over the entire house to check for any speck of dust, and if she found any, we heard about it. She would turn to my father and growl, "Martin, what kind of woman did you marry? She can't even keep her house clean!" Sometimes she inspected me, and after close scrutiny, she barked at my mother, "You're not feeding Clive enough, Maureen. You've got to feed this boy!" When I got a little older, I realized why my father was so rigid and demanding. He

My mother the actress

never felt that he could measure up to his mother's expectations, and he communicated the same unrealistic demands to my mother and the children. He was a brilliant engineer and businessman, and he had a sincere desire to care for his family, but no amount of success seemed to fill the void in his heart.

Before her marriage to my father, my mother was a gifted actress. She performed in the theater, from Shakespeare to children's plays. She was a strikingly beautiful woman— blonde with green eyes, the picture of a princess. Her favorite role was Wendy in *Peter Pan,* and today, at 75, she can still quote passages from Shakespeare's plays.

It's a Gift

When I was six, my mother prepared for a dinner party. As usual, I was loitering in the kitchen because I wanted to experience the flavors and aromas of everything she was making. In the middle of her preparation, she was called to the phone in another room. I looked in the refrigerator for a snack and found a jar of Beluga caviar she intended to use for caviar blinis that night. I tasted it, and I loved it so much that I ate the whole jar!

You've heard the old saying, "If you can't stand the heat, get out of the kitchen." From the time I was a little boy, I've never gotten out of the kitchen. I love the challenge, the creativity of cooking, and the incredible variety of tastes. I grew up with exotic and unique flavors as a part of my daily life. South Africa is the crossroads of many cultures. In the restaurants and bakeries, as well as in our home, my mother made sure that we experienced the foods of India, Britain, France, Holland, and Portugal. Even as a young child, I was aware that I had a gift of taste and smell. (I love guessing ladies' perfumes. I can tell a lady what perfume she's wearing even if we're in a room of 100 others who are wearing different, competing fragrances.) At home, one of our servants, Peter, had been with our family since before my father was born. He became my mother's assistant chef. One of my most vivid memories of Peter is that he often cooked chicken in a way that still makes my mouth water.

He rubbed the chicken with his blend of spices and roasted it. When it was done, he set it aside to rest for about 30 minutes, and I often pinched off the "parson's nose" and enjoyed the crispy, delicious flavor.

One of my better days at school

I'm thankful my mother let me learn from her about cooking because I didn't excel in the classroom. I'm at best a C student, and my lack of school success was quite a challenge for my dad. My father was exceptionally bright, and he had been an outstanding student. He expected me to be as good a student as he had been, and when my grades came in as C's and D's, he expressed his displeasure in no uncertain terms! He put me at the desk in our home for hours at a time, and when I failed to sufficiently concentrate on my studies, he sometimes beat me. When beatings failed to produce the desired results, he sent me to boarding school. I felt like a colossal failure. I have vivid and terrible memories of Sunday nights and the end of summer break because I dreaded school starting the next day.

Besides cooking, my other love was sports. I was captain of our school's swimming team and an opening bowler for my cricket team. For those who don't know, a bowler is like a pitcher in baseball. I practiced for hours in our backyard by throwing at a rainwater drainpipe between two windows. I had to be very accurate or glass would be shattered. (To be honest, windows had to be replaced a few times.) I especially enjoyed summer vacations in Plettenberg Bay because I went fishing every day and caught elf, mussel crackers, and lionfish.

Our family was selectively kosher at home, and our Jewish roots and traditions were important to us. We celebrated the festivals, and we attended synagogue whenever we could. I really enjoyed it. Like every Jewish boy, my bar mitzvah occurred when I turned 13. Traditionally, the Bible passage read for a boy's transition to manhood is simply the next text in the liturgical calendar. The text read for my bar mitzvah was a paragraph in Leviticus 12 about women purifying themselves after their menstrual cycle! The passages for other young men in our family told of bold men of faith and courage. Mine was a bit different. Oh, well.

My talents and personality reflect my mother's flare for creativity rather than my father's engineering skills. If it weren't for my mother and her love of cooking, I don't know where I'd be today. I intuitively grasped the principles of cooking, and with that foundation, I developed a desire to experiment in the kitchen. Beyond my gift of smell and taste and the influence of my mother's skill in the kitchen, I love to cook because it allows me to spend time with people, and people fascinate me.

To me, cooking is a combination of art and sport. I love the creativity and complexity of preparing something that's beyond anyone's expectations, and I revel in the risk of making it all come together in just the right way at just the right time. Every aspect of the meal—from shopping for the freshest ingredients . . . to preparing the food . . . to presenting the dishes . . . to meaningful conversations with friends and family—inspires and challenges me. Even disasters can be turned into something special. I call it "the oops factor." With a little imagination and optimism, a mistake can be salvaged—and the dish may even become a new masterpiece. Actually, some of the world's most famous dishes—such as Crepe Suzette, Beef Wellington, and Steak Diane—were created this way.

The Surprise Chef

Though I wasn't a good student, my father still wanted me to go to college. He warned me, though, that if I didn't make good grades, he would send me to the army. I couldn't imagine he was serious, but after six months of pitifully low grades, I got home one day to find that my bag was packed and sitting in my father's car. In the freezing cold of mid-winter, I joined the 4th South African Infantry in Middleburg.

I was miserable in the army. In the first weeks with the infantry, the routine and drudgery bored me to death. Soon, I learned that I was one of 17 Jewish young men in our company. We wanted the army to provide kosher meals for us, and for some strange reason, the men picked me to be their spokesman. I went to see the Captain and asked him to provide a kosher chef for us. At that time, the law required the army to provide a kosher chef for Jewish soldiers, so he agreed to find one for us. Two days later, the Captain told me that he was unable to find a chef. I don't know why I said it, but instantly I volunteered, "Sir, I can cook."

"Have you cooked before?" he asked.

Though I had only cooked breakfasts for my family and watched my mother cook, I told him confidently, "Yes, sir. I have."

He agreed to let me be the chef, but he told me that I'd still have to complete basic training. As soon as I left the Captain's office, I ran to the pay phone to call home and get some recipes. My mother wasn't home, but Peter answered. He didn't speak much English, but I was able to communicate that I needed the recipe for his delicious roasted chicken and a few other dishes. A few days later, my first meal as a chef was Peter's famous chicken. When I took it out of the oven, I was proud of it, but when I cut a slice, I could see that it wasn't done. I threw it in the fryer to finish it (which is the best way to cover up cooking mistakes—frying can make anything taste good), and the men enjoyed it. Later I talked to my mother, and she sent me a few of her recipes I could use.

My on-the-job training as a chef received an additional boost because the butcher for Middleburg was a rabbi. He brought meat every Friday morning and often stayed to talk to me about what it means to be Jewish and observe kosher laws. I must admit that I'm not sure how kosher I cooked, but people loved everything that came from my kitchen. After knowing him a few weeks, the rabbi and his wife invited all 17 of us to town on Friday evening for Shabbat: services at the synagogue and dinner at their house. The army didn't provide us with a truck, so we walked about a mile to town every Friday. In our interactions, the rabbi reinforced my perception of the special role of Jews. For him, it wasn't about the foods. Kosher cooking was an expression of God's unique place and purpose for the Jewish people. He gave me confidence so that I have never been ashamed of my race, faith, or culture.

The Jewish soldiers enjoyed the food I prepared for them, and soon the officers in our unit joined the men in my serving line. I learned that other men in our unit would barter for meals I cooked. To get through basic training, I cooked meals for the man who cleaned rifles best if he would clean mine, I swapped meals for the one who spotlessly polished shoes if he would polish mine, and I offered meals to the soldier who made his bed to perfection if he would make mine. With bartered services, I passed inspections with flying colors! This arrangement worked for me, and by the looks on their faces as they ate, it worked for them, too. After basic training, I was assigned to Defense Headquarters in Pretoria, where, in addition to my duties as a chef, a friend asked me to sit in as a DJ on Friday and Saturday nights. I wasn't as skilled on stage as my mother, but I got to perform a bit in my own way.

The nine months as a chef in the army gave me confidence that I could make a living in the hotel and restaurant business. I had received countless negative messages during my childhood, but suddenly, people valued my abilities and me. I can't overstate the impact their affirmations had on me. For years, I had wandered without confidence, but now people looked to me for excellence and leadership. I had been lost; now I had been found.

The Taste of a New Direction

I had always been fascinated with fine dining and great hotels. For years, my family had visited the Beacon Island Hotel, one of the most gorgeous hotels in the world, at Plettenberg Bay. Every time we went there, I walked through the dining rooms, marveling at the gracious hospitality and their commitment to excellence. From the first day I experienced the Beacon Island Hotel, I wanted to be a part of something just as grand and elegant. Now, with my successful stint in the army, my vision of the future began to take shape. As soon as I was mustered out of the army, I announced to my parents that I wanted to go to school in hotel and restaurant management.

My father had always envisioned his sons as doctors, attorneys, or engineers. There's no doubt that my performance in school gave him a strong dose of reality, so when I showed some skill and passion for hotel and restaurant management, he agreed to let me go. My mother was genuinely thrilled for me. The best schools were in Lucerne, Switzerland, and London, England. At the time, Britain had an agreement with its former colonies to offer educational opportunities at the same tuition previously offered under the colonial system. I would have loved to go to Lucerne, but I'd have to learn French, and besides, the school in England was much less expensive. As a young man of 18, I flew to London and enrolled in Cassio College. My father had done some business with a man who lived in London. He and his wife invited me to live with them at the beginning of the first term. I lived there for about four months, and then I moved into the YMCA.

In stark contrast to my earlier academic career, I loved college. I devoured every subject in hotel and restaurant management, and I excelled. Shockingly, I was named Student of the Year—a far cry from the string of dismal failures I had suffered in the past! To get experience, students worked in hotels and restaurants in London. I loved working in little restaurants. The owners paid me almost nothing, but the experience was incredibly valuable.

I saw the business from every person's point of view: the owner, the chef, the waiter, the busboy, and the guest. Every day, the staff had to work together to produce extraordinary dishes. It was addictive! We took raw material, worked our magic in the kitchen to prepare and present a distinctive meal, and tried to give people something they'd never forget. That was our goal, and to a large extent, we fulfilled it. The reward of the restaurant business isn't money; it's when a guest puts down his fork, smiles, and says, "Wow, that was really good!"

At one point, I worked at a little Italian restaurant in Watford, the hometown of Elton John. The kitchen was tiny, and the owner was huge, tough, and demanding. He regularly chewed out the cooks and wait staff for the smallest infraction. One day he was away from the kitchen, and a waiter brought me an order from a regular customer who wanted his usual seafood dish, which wasn't an item found on the menu. I didn't know how to make it, but that was no problem. I threw together some tomatoes, olive oil, spices, red peppers, seafood, and pasta, and I sent it out. The waiter set the plate in front of the guest, and he complained, "That's not what I ordered."

The waiter tried to be brave and said, "Go ahead and try it. You'll like it."

The man took a bite. In a few seconds, his demeanor completely changed. He looked up at the waiter and said, "This is fantastic!" The waiter almost ran back into the kitchen to tell me the guest was delighted with the dish. There's no better feeling for a cook or a chef, and it was another lesson for me to learn: Even if you don't know exactly what to do, follow your instincts and do something special. Some of the most renowned recipes have come occurred when the chef was under intense pressure (or even by mistake), and they proved to be delicious.

During the break after my first year in school, I traveled to Germany and France to visit the vineyards. It was there that I fell in love with wine. At the time, I knew very little about wine. In fact, if red and white wine weren't different colors, I couldn't have told them apart. Walking in the vineyards that summer, watching the winemakers at work, and sampling their wines opened a new world for me. The process of taking grapes from the vine to age in bottles captured my imagination and my heart. I soon realized that winemaking truly is an art. Two vineyards may be next to each other and grow the same variety of grapes, but the differences in their winemaking process produces wines with subtle but distinctly different flavors. Every year produces a different vintage affected by the weather conditions and decisions made by the winemaker that particular year . . . creativity at its highest.

I enjoyed all wines, but champagne particularly fascinated me. Soon I learned again that it's not about *what* you know; it's about *who* you know. I developed a relationship with the director of the Comité Interprofessionnel du Vin de Champagne, and he invited me to pick grapes in Avize. I was paid only about 10 Francs a day, which is about a dollar, but I thoroughly enjoyed being part of the process of producing some of the finest champagne in the world.

Vineyard in Champagne near Aviz

When the summer break came along after my second year at college, a friend invited me to spend several weeks at his home in St. Tropez in the south of France. My friend traveled to London part of that summer, and while he was away, I had the run of his home. One day, he called to tell me that a friend of the family, Judy Navia, was coming for visit from Geneva with her two children and would soon return home to New York. Her husband had died not long before, and she needed some time away from home. For those two weeks, she went with me to the market each morning, and I cooked for her and her children. This was my first independent cooking experience, and I thoroughly enjoyed it.

Judy and her children left St. Tropez about the same time I had to go back to school. We said "goodbye," and I assumed I'd never hear from her again. A couple of months later, I was back in London. One night, at 3:00 in the morning, I received a phone call from my mother in New York. (My family had moved there not long before to escape the violence that was gripping South Africa as racial equality replaced apartheid.) In an excited voice, she said, "Tell me what happened in the south of France. And what do you know about Halloween?"

I tried to clear my head, and I asked, "What . . . what do you mean?"

She explained, "A lady and her children came to our door for something called 'Trick or Treat.' We talked for a few minutes, and she recognized my accent. I told her I was from South Africa, and she said she knew a lovely young man from South Africa. She met him at St. Tropez last summer. I asked, 'What's his name?' She replied, 'Clive Berkman.' I almost fainted and told her, 'That's my son!' "

New York. If Only Temporarily

After graduating from Cassio College, I planned on getting a masters degree. However, my high school sweetheart, Lynn, invited me to go to New York with her. My parents were already there, and I thought Lynn was the girl of my dreams. With stars in my eyes, I turn my back on higher education and moved to New York. After only a month in the city, though, she decided she didn't like New York or me, so she moved to Los Angeles. Suddenly rudderless, I needed a job, and I wanted to reconnect with my dad, so I went to work for him in his wholesale grocery and supply business. I certainly hadn't lost my passion for the restaurant business. I just needed a place to earn a few dollars while I decided my next move.

As I walked the streets of New York and watched people, I had an idea. People love good food, but they're too busy to spend time preparing it. I could create a business to make great food they could pick up on the way home. I could make delicious sauces and pasta. All they had to do was warm it up when they got home, and they'd have a feast. At that time, there were only two or three pasta machines in all of New York. I began investigating which machines I'd buy in Italy and bring back to my operation, how to package sauces, and how to market our cuisine to New Yorkers. I spent weeks analyzing the possibilities and pursuing options. (My mother always said I was a dreamer.)

Though I was only 23 and had never owned a business, I was certain this concept would be a big hit. Things started taking shape, and I set up a meeting with executives from a company that was going to design the packaging for our products. By now, winter had settled over the city. The morning of my meeting, I got up early and got dressed. I was very excited about the possibilities of this new venture. I commuted into the city for the appointment, but snow from the night before made my 45-minute trip last two hours. I was late! I parked underground and ran toward the building where people were waiting for me. I tried to make it across the street as a light turned red, but I realized I wasn't going to make it. I tried to get back to the curb, but I slipped on the slush and slid into the gutter. As I lay there, the cars and buses didn't even stop. They sped past me like I was a piece of rubbish. Dripping wet and freezing, I climbed up onto the sidewalk. I was furious. I walked resolutely into my meeting and told them I'd changed my mind. The deal was off. If that was life in New York, I didn't want any part of it. I wanted to find a place where I belonged, and that certainly wasn't New York. I went home and told my parents that I was leaving the next day. My father asked, "Where are you going?"

I declared confidently, "To Miami."

I wanted out of New York as soon as possible. My father gave me a Chevy Nova and $2000. At 4:00 the next morning—less than 18 hours after I was supposed to have a pivotal meeting to launch a new business—I was on the road to South Florida. Even now, when I drive across the George Washington Bridge, those old feelings of anger and desperation come flooding back into my memory. At the time, I had to find a different life, and I hoped Miami would be a good place to start again.

Learning the Business

I stayed with some cousins for a few weeks in Miami and got a job as an assistant maitre d' at the new Bonaventure Country Club for $125 a week. I told the manager that I wanted to be more involved, so I came in early to help cook breakfast, I stayed to help prepare for lunch, and then went home to take a nap before my shift as a maitre d' in the evening. It was great being on my own and working hard, but I wanted a more significant role in restaurant management.

One night only a few months after arriving in Miami, a friend who also worked at the restaurant went with me to Denny's late at night after work. As we sat in a booth eating a late-night breakfast, I told my friend that I wanted to find a new job. I complained about being overworked and underpaid, and I wanted more of a challenge. After a few minutes, I felt a tap on my shoulder. The man in the next booth peered over at me and said, "Are you in the restaurant business?"

"Yes," I said, not knowing what he had overheard but quickly replaying the conversation in my mind.

"Here's my card," he told me. "Call me tomorrow. I may have something for you."

It didn't take me long. I called him early the next morning and made an appointment to see him before lunch. He asked about my experience, and then he said, "I want you to call Victor Broceaux. He has an opening."

The next day, I met Victor at his restaurant. Victor is from the Basque region bordering Spain and France. He was opening a new restaurant, Reflections on the Bay, in the Miami Marina. The restaurant was part of Restaurant Associates, which had also operated The Four Seasons, La Fonda del Sol, Mama Leoni's, La Brasserie, the restaurant at the top of Rockefeller Plaza, and many others in New York. He asked some questions about my background and experience. He was European and I was a South African trained in Europe, so we hit it off at once. We spoke the same language about food and wine, and we instinctively understood each other. After a few minutes, he told me, "You're a little too young for the job I have in mind for you, but I'm going to take you under my wing and give you a chance—but you'd better listen to me. Do you understand?"

Victor, my mentor, and me

Victor was a small man, but he was packed with dynamite. When he told me I needed to listen to him, I took him seriously. He was tough as nails, and I worked my tail off for him. I was thrilled to work for a talented, determined man as he opened a fine restaurant. Whatever he needed, I got it done for him. I found a supplier for rare mushrooms, discovered the best markets where we could buy produce, picked out tablecloths, and ran any errands Victor had for me. Soon, I earned Victor's confidence.

We opened Reflections, but within six months, we went through three general managers and two chefs. I worked more closely with Victor than anyone, and I knew the standards he set for the restaurant. When our manager and chef didn't perform the way they should, I told Victor. To say the least, I wasn't the favorite of some people in our restaurant. They saw me as a threat, and to be honest, I was exactly that.

One of the eye-opening experiences of those first months at Reflections was that drug dealers frequented our restaurant. Miami has long been one of the most important doors to the drug trade from South America. From time to time, a group of men booked a back room and hired a waiter for the evening. These people dropped big money. At first, I wondered who they were. One of the waiters explained what was going on, and soon I realized that these men expected special treatment—and they got it.

After the massive turnover of top staff, Restaurant Associates hired a new team to run the restaurant. Victor boasted to them about my hard work, experience, and commitment to excellence, so the corporate executives sent me to New York to interview with the general manager of La Brasserie. There, the manager offered me the job of assistant manager. I felt honored and I wanted to take the job, but the last place I wanted to live was New York. I turned down the offer and returned to Miami. When I walked in the door of Reflections the next day, the new restaurant general manager growled at me, "Where have you been? We've been looking for you."

Victor, I soon learned, hadn't cleared my trip to New York with the general manager. I tried to explain, "Victor set up the job interview for me in New York."

"Then you'd better take the job," he growled, "because you don't have one here." He fired me on the spot.

I was angry, but I wasn't going to remain on the sidelines. I called Walt Larson, a man who had come to Reflections several times to check us out for Club Corporation of America, a company which manages private clubs. Walt immediately hired me as the service director for Banker's Club of Miami, so I had a new job the day I was fired.

Within a few months, Walt, the chef, and I became a regional team operating several restaurants in the area. CCA has some of the highest service standards in the industry. In my work with Victor, I learned about great food. In my work with Walt, I learned how to give guests exemplary service.

Charley's

One day I was at Menu Men in Miami having our menus printed. The owner, who had become a friend of mine, answered the phone, and after a few minutes of conversation, he turned to me and asked, "Clive, do you have a resume?"

"For what?" I asked incredulously. I wondered why in the world would he ask me that question. I was just having menus printed, and you don't need a resume for that.

He explained, "The man on the phone, Harry, is a head-hunter in Houston who's looking for someone to be the general manager in one of the top restaurants in town. He told me what kind of person he's looking for, and I think you're the guy."

I shook my head and told him, "No, I'm not really interested. I like it here, and I don't want to move."

He wouldn't take "no" for an answer. I told him that I didn't have a resume, but he insisted that I tell him my credentials and experience so he could create one for me while I stood there waiting for my menus to be printed. Immediately, he faxed my freshly minted resume to Harry, and the next day, he called me. A few days later, I flew to Houston to meet with Harry and see the restaurant, Charley's 517.

In 1982, I was only 25, but I grew a mustache so I would look a bit older. The interview for the general manager's job went well. They liked my perspectives and tastes in food and wine. Charley's was, indeed, a very fine restaurant in downtown Houston. It was located in the theater district, and much of its business came from people who attended shows and cultural events at the Alley Theater, Jones Hall, and the Music Hall (which became the Hobby Theater) a few blocks from Charley's.

A very special guest

I flew back to Miami and planned to return to my job. I really had no intentions of taking the role at Charley's. Houston didn't seem to compare with the glitz and glamour of New York and Miami, but the people at Charley's were persistent. They asked me to come back, and when I met with them again, they offered me a package I couldn't refuse.

I moved to Houston and began a role for which I'd been preparing all my life. The president of the company that owned Charley's had a passion to build the restaurant's wine list to be one of the best in the world. We excavated the ground under the restaurant to build

The Wine Cellar at Charley's 517

The Wine Cellar, and in only three years, we had 20,000 bottles of the finest wines in the world. I traveled to all the great vineyards of France and America to find the best wines and the finest vintages. To understand and appreciate fine wines, a person has to visit the most prestigious vineyards, understand the winemaking process, and extensively research each vintage. We bought individual bottles and lots of bottles at auction in London at Christie's and Sotheby's. Among the finest in our vertical collections were Chateau Margaux, Chateau Lafite Rothschild, Chateau Lynch Bages, Chateau Leoville Barton, and Chateau Pichon Lalande. In fact, we had all the great vintages of Chateau Margaux going back to 1899. We bought rare bottles of small California vineyards, such as Chateau Montelena Chardonnay, which won the Paris Exposition of 1973, and Stony Hill Chardonnay. We wanted depth in our list of French wines, and we wanted an exceptional variety of California wines.

My passion for wine found a perfect fit with the president's vision for The Wine Cellar. Our goal was to win *Wine Spectator* magazine's Grand Award, the top wine award in the world. We won it in 1985, only our third year, and we won every year until 1997. Only three restaurants in Texas have ever won the award, so we were proud to receive the honor. The prestigious award established our restaurant as one of the premier restaurants in Houston. We often received the compliment that we were the best restaurant in downtown Houston. I replied, "Thank you," but I thought, *Actually, we're the only restaurant in downtown Houston, so it's not hard to be the best.*

The next year, the French government sponsored a wine tasting competition, and I won the award for our region of the United States. They flew all the regional finalists to New York for the national tasting. The night before the competition, I caught a cold. It's very difficult to distinguish flavors and smells with a nasty head cold. Needless to say, I didn't win, but it was still a great experience.

Every day at Charley's was exciting. I made a point of learning things about our guests so I could make each visit special. If you asked people about our restaurant in those days, most of them would smile and say something like, "Yes, I remember it well. I had some wonderful times there. The food, the wine, the service . . . everything was memorable!"

One of the principles that drove us is that we knew we could overcome any problem except a bad first impression. If our guests' food wasn't good, we could cook them a new meal and give it to them without charge. If they didn't like their wine, we could open a new bottle for them. But if we didn't impress them the instant they got out of their car and stepped into the restaurant, we couldn't recover from the blunder. To achieve that level of service, I became, I'm afraid, my grandmother. Every day, I inspected our wait staff, our valets, and every detail of presentation of the restaurant. And too often, I treated my staff the same way my grandmother treated us. I barked corrections until they did it right—by my standards of what was right, of course. I wanted each of the pieces of silverware to be a thumbprint from the edge of the table. I insisted that the salt and pepper be placed exactly in the same place on each table, and each glass had to be perfectly spotless. Some people might ask why I was such a stickler for perfection. My answer is that an architect will examine the construction and layout of the building, an accountant will scrutinize the itemization of the bill, an interior decorator will see if the pictures are straight or crooked, and a doctor will examine the cleanliness of the room. No single guest will notice *all* of these, but everyone will notice *something*. It's our job—our responsibility and our privilege—to serve people so well that everyone is impressed, no matter which detail he or she examines closely.

We trained our staff to always call people "guests," not "customers." We never asked, "Can I get something for you?" Of course we *can*. That's why we were there. The appropriate question is, "May I get something for you?" This wording invites the guest to request our services.

I was tough on our staff, but they knew I valued them. Years later, I realized I could have spoken to them with far more grace, but at the time, I hadn't yet experienced grace myself. I couldn't give them something I didn't possess. Our staff sometimes said, "When you work at a place like this, you're not expected to make a mistake."

I hate to admit it, but sometimes I was over the top in my demands on them. A few times, when a table wasn't set perfectly before we opened for the evening, I growled my disapproval at the person who set the table and yanked the tablecloth, sending knives, forks, spoons, salt, pepper, napkins, and the vase of flowers flying! I wanted to make a point, and it was the only way I knew how. One night, a member of our wait staff was serving guests at Table 19 near the front door. At the exact moment he opened the door to the kitchen to pick up the food, I yelled an expletive at one of the cooks. Everybody in the entire dining room heard me. And my anger got the best of me yet another time. One of our cooks was a large, muscular man about 6 feet 3 inches tall. One particular evening, we had a heated argument. After a few minutes, he had had enough of my demands, and he grabbed a knife. The look in his eye told me he wasn't thinking of using it to chop vegetables! I'm only 5 feet 7 inches tall, but grabbed his arm and snarled, "You'd better know what you're going to do with that knife!" After a few seconds, he put it down. (I guess he realized it wasn't worth going to prison to prove his point.) I'm certainly not proud of the volcano of anger that erupted from time to time. These episodes were outward signs of a deep hurt that had never been healed.

The staff

In spite of my demands on our staff, we developed some wonderful relationships. Not long ago, I was having dinner at the Capital Grill in Houston, and I saw two men who used to be waiters at Charley's. One of them told me with a smile, "Clive, my life was totally changed because of you. Everything I've ever learned about the restaurant business I learned from you." And the other told me, "That's true for me, too. I looked you up on your web site. You've always been in my heart since our time together at Charley's. At the time, I thought you were the hardest boss I'd ever had, but since then, I've realized that you've had an impact on me that can't be measured. You taught me

the value of doing things right. I haven't learned anything new since I left you and Charley's."
I appreciate their kind words.

Houston, We Have a Problem

In the mid-80's the bottom dropped out of the oil market, and at the time, Houston's economy was very dependent on oil. The company decided to sell some of the restaurants, including Charley's. The president of the company was as emotionally invested in Charley's as I was, so he asked me if I'd like to be his partner to buy the restaurant. I agreed, and we arranged the financing. In 1986, we signed the papers to buy it, and the next Sunday, I got married to my sweetheart, Darcee. It was a busy week.

I was totally devoted to the restaurant business, but I was also devoted to my marriage with Darcee. After about a year, she got pregnant. When our son Ian was born, I was the happiest father in the world. Darcee was a terrific mother, but a few days after Ian's first birthday, she announced she was leaving me. Looking back, I should have seen it coming, but at the time, I was devastated. The hurt made me more defensive, and I was determined to do two things: never put my heart in anyone's hands, and pour my entire life into the restaurant business where I felt most comfortable and confident.

Ian's first day in the kitchen with Loretta Phoenix

I've got much of my mother in me, so at Charley's we created "performances" that entertained people with the finest foods and wines. We hosted vintner dinners showcasing the wines of the 50's, 60's, and 70's, we taught various cooking and wine classes, and we donated dinners to various organizations and charities. Our gift to the Leukemia & Lymphoma Society was dinner for 20 people auctioned by the charity. One year, Mike Munchak of the Houston Oilers bought the dinners at the auction. A few months later, he brought his entire offensive line, first and second teams, and these enormous men ate more than any people we ever served! Our 50's theme was titled "Poodle Skirts and Flattops." Two of the most exquisite and elegant dinners at Charley's were times when we featured the wines of Chateau Margaux and Chateau Lafite Rothschild. We also catered an election night dinner for George and Barbara Bush, hosted baseball legend Yogi Berra, and served dignitaries from all walks of life. Throughout our history at Charley's, we created special moments people enjoyed. Each extravagant event and private dinner was a challenge and a joy. (You'll find many of these events along with their menus and recipes in the book in the section titled "Vintner Dinners.")

For me, the signposts of great memories are empty wine bottles. I used to keep empty bottles around the restaurant, and people sometimes looked at me like I was crazy to keep them. I explained that full bottles have the potential to tell a story, but empty bottles already have a wonderful story to tell. Each empty bottle speaks of a special moment in a person's life. When I pick up a particular bottle, I remember the look on a couple's face the night he proposed to her, the proud parents of a graduate, a family celebrating a daughter's 21st birthday, or any of a thousand other specific memories of men and women, young and old, who celebrated with us. When I gave people tours of The Wine Cellar, I could show them an unopened bottle of Vosne Romanee La Tache 1963 and tell them about my trip to France to buy it and bring it back. But I could also show them an empty bottle of Chateau Lafite Rothschild 1961 and explain that we served a young couple that was to be married the next week. That night we served them marinated quail, and when we opened the bottle, the aroma filled the room with cedar and berry. The couple had a magical, romantic evening with us. I love telling those stories because they remind me of the delight on people's faces.

We looked for ways to make every meal a memorable occasion. When the Astros traded for All Star pitcher Randy Johnson in July of 1998, he was an instant sensation in the city. I found out that Johnson's favorite dessert was cheesecake. After each time Johnson pitched, we adjusted the price of a slice of cheesecake to match his most recently calculated ERA (Earned Run Average), and we posted it every day on a huge sign out front.

When the bottom dropped out of the oil market and the price of a barrel plummeted near $10, the economy of Houston suffered terribly. Suddenly, lavish expense accounts dried up as CFOs put the clamps on executive spending. We offered a lunch menu at the current price of a barrel of oil. It was a deal, and for hungry executives, a deal they could really enjoy. Like Randy Johnson's ERA, we posted the price of a barrel of oil each day out-side the restaurant to promote our unique lunch deal.

Day after day, we had the incredible privilege of providing a special atmosphere for people to celebrate birthdays, anniversaries, engagements, graduations, promotions, and any other occasion that meant a lot to them. Even today, people come up to me and thank me for the wonderful time they had on their special occasions. They remember that night because we did everything possible to make a moment they'd never forget. All of our shop-ping for the best food and wine, our hours of preparation and our attention to detail, our training of the staff, and our commitment to excellence in food, wine, and service—all of it is well worth it when someone tells me that an evening in Charley's was a milestone in their marriage or their family. Being a part of these memories . . . that's a treat.

Of course, not all of my memories of Charley's are delightful. One night our valet parked our guests' cars on the street. The Houston Police determined that they were all parked illegally, so they towed them all away. There were a lot of surprised and unhappy guests that night! Another time, a cold front blew into the city, and many of the ladies wore their mink coats that night. The front wasn't predicted, so we didn't have enough staff for parking and checking coats. I was out of the restaurant for a few hours, and when I came back, we had to scramble to have our valets doing double duty, checking coats and parking cars, too. Later, a couple finished their meal and got up to leave. The wife handed her claim stub to the valet to get her coat, but the mink was gone! It took us a while, but we tracked it down and got it back to her. She was very gracious about it.

In 1995, we were part of Houston's annual International Festival. One morning during the event, I was in a golf cart near City Hall where the tents were set up. The wind was blowing from the north up Louisiana Street, and I smelled smoke. I commented rather dispassionately, "Something's on fire." As we drove the cart down the street, the smoke got thicker. We arrived at Charley's at the same moment the fire trucks pulled up with their sirens blaring. Charley's was on fire!

The next hours were agonizing. As firemen called out orders and hosed down the flames, I paced back and forth in front of the restaurant. Everything I had worked for and treasured was going up in smoke. In the afternoon, a local television news crew asked me for an interview. They placed me so that the smoke billowed up behind me, and they asked

Reopening Charley's after the fire

me how I felt about the fire. The news that night showed me, distraught with tears running down my cheeks, saying, "It meant the world to me. It was my whole life."

Rebuilding and reopening the restaurant took three long months. Like everyone who experiences traumatic events, I felt shaken by the daunting realization that a catastrophe could occur at any time without warning, and the things I held onto tightly could vanish in an instant. I felt discouraged and depressed. To be sure that I didn't have all my eggs in one basket, I started other businesses. Crème de la Crème Catering specialized in providing fine dinners for intimate events in homes in the upscale part of Houston. We also did backstage catering for performers at Cynthia Woods Mitchell Pavilion, the Alley Theater, and Jones Hall. I was incredibly busy.

Filling the Empty Place

In 1997, we changed the name of the restaurant to Clive's, and we changed the concept from a formal, traditional, white-table cloth restaurant to a trendy grill. The grand reopening occurred on my 40th birthday. The following year was the best we'd ever had. Downtown Houston had recovered from the collapse of the oil market, and it was booming. The city hosted The Power of Houston, an extravaganza that attracted hundreds of thousands to the city. Things were going well, but I still felt a gnawing emptiness, and success wasn't enough to fill it.

For about three years, I had worked with Carlos St. Mary on ad placements for the restaurant. One day in 1999, I went to his office for a marketing meeting. Carlos had seen me at my best and at my worst. That day, he decided it was time to say something about my anger and my need to control every situation. After we met, he came outside and said, "Hey Clive, if I can use one of your Jewish words, I'd say that you don't have any *shalom* in your life."

I tried to blow him off like I'd blown off everybody else who had ever tried to talk to me about the hurt and anger they saw in me. I waved him off as if to say, "You don't know what you're talking about," but Carlos persisted, "No, Clive. You have everything anyone could want. Your name is on the front of one of the finest restaurants in town, you travel the world, and you have financial success, but you don't have any peace."

For some reason, Carlos's combination of honesty and kindness hit a nerve. I lowered my guard and answered, "Yeah, you're kind of right. I have a lot of things, but not what I really want. I want a wonderful marriage, but I'm divorced. I want a nice little restaurant that isn't a strain, but Clive's drains me. I want a warm, loving family, but I feel alone. You're right, Carlos. I don't have any peace."

Carlos looked at me and said, "Clive, I've got an answer for you."

I assumed he was talking about counseling. After the fire, I had been emotionally devastated. I had gone to a counselor for a couple of years, and I had taken medications for depression during that time. After a while, though, the counselor told me I was doing well enough so I didn't need to see him any more. Now, I thought Carlos was going to tell me I needed to go back into therapy. I asked, "What answer are you talking about?"

"A relationship with Jesus Christ," he said without flinching.

His words were like putting a match to a stick of dynamite. I barked, "Absolutely not! There's no way. You're crazy."

"Why not?" he asked calmly.

I stared at him a few seconds before I answered: "Carlos, in case you've forgotten, I'm Jewish."

He smiled and without missing a beat he told me, "So was Jesus." He let that sink in for a second, and then he asked, "Do you believe in God?"

"Yeah," I responded a bit defensively. "I believe there's a Creator."

"Then open your heart to him." With that, Carlos shook my hand and walked away.

I wasn't thrilled about the conversation with Carlos, but something about it fascinated me. Later that day, I was on my way to another meeting, and I picked up my cell phone and called him. When he answered, I acted like our conversation was still going on: "Buy me a Bible."

He laughed, "Clive, you don't have a Bible?"

"No," I tried to explain. "I'm Jewish. What would I need with a Bible? The rabbi read to us in synagogue."

The next day, Carlos called to tell me that he had a Bible for me. His office was right around the corner from where I lived, and for several weeks, I went to his office every day. He simply opened the Bible to various places and read about the love of God, the importance of trusting God, and the fact that God has a plan for our lives. I had never heard or read the passages like these before—or at least, I never had listened when the rabbi read them. During all this time, Carlos never tried to force anything on me in any way. He just read to me about the character and personality of God, and he let me know he cared about me. Carlos always left me with a question to think about.

The week before Memorial Day, I was at the restaurant, and I saw two ladies who had been on the board of the Food and Wine Society with me. I had known them for 15 years, so they had seen me in the good times and the bad. After a few minutes of conversation, one of them looked at me and asked in a voice of surprise, "Clive, what's going on with you? Something's different. You seem more relaxed, maybe . . . at peace."

I wondered what she was talking about. I replied, "Well, I'm reading the Bible, and I'm trying to find out who Jesus is. That's the only thing that's different."

Both ladies looked shocked. Simultaneously, they blurted out, "But you're Jewish!"

When I was growing up, parents in our community warned the kids to stay away from anybody who talks about Jesus, because "he was a kook." He was worse than a rebel; he was insane. In their opinion, no good could come from reading or talking about him. They would say, "We're Jewish, and we don't mix with Gentiles." Now, though, I was very interested in finding out more about Jesus. "Yeah, but I'm fascinated by this man Jesus," I explained. "I don't know much about him, but I'm learning."

After they left, another lady who had overheard our conversation asked, "Where do you go to church, Clive?"

"Church?" I asked, making a face of disgust. "Why would I go to church? Jews go to synagogue."

She wasn't deterred. "Don't you want to go?"

"No, not really."

She continued bravely, "If you ever want to go, I recommend Second Baptist. That's where I go. I think you'd enjoy it."

"Where is it?" I asked.

She explained where the church is located, and I laughed. I explained, "I remember when they were building it. I thought it was a huge mosque."

She was a bulldog who wouldn't let go. "Well, you really ought to go. I think you'd like it a lot."

I was softening a bit. "Who's your main guy there?"

"Our pastor?"

"Yeah, your pastor."

"His name is Ed Young."

"Okay," I told her. "Give him my number. If he wants me to come, he needs to call me."

She replied, "Oh Clive, why don't you just come and see what it's like."

I'm sure she thought that was the end of any conversation we'd ever have about God and church.

The very next night, the Morrises, a couple who often visited our restaurant, came in. Almost immediately, Mrs. Morris looked at me closely and asked, "Clive, are you in love?"

I laughed. "Why would you ask me a question like that?"

She smiled, "Because you have the look of someone who is in love, that's why."

"That's very odd," I mused out loud. "Last night, someone said almost exactly the same thing to me." I paused a second, and then explained, "I'm trying to find out who Jesus is."

She immediately asked, "Are you going to church?"

I thought, *Here we go again!* I replied, "No, I'm not going to church—and I have no intentions to *ever* go."

She completely disregarded my defensiveness. "Let me recommend one to you," she offered. "Second Baptist Church is wonderful. Have you heard of it?"

"Yes," I told her. "I'll think about it."

The next night, Carlos took me to dinner with a man who was getting married a week or so later. As we talked, the man told me he met his fiancée at a Bible study at Second Baptist Church.

Once, I could easily forget it. Twice, I was paying attention. But when someone told me about Second Baptist Church the third day in a row, I knew something very strange was going on. I decided to go the next Sunday, but I certainly didn't want to look like a fool on my first visit, so I drove over to the church on Saturday afternoon to get my bearings. I spotted a good place to park and walked around until I found the worship center. A lot of people know me in Houston, and I didn't want to draw attention to myself by looking foolish. The Saturday scouting trip helped me find my way. Then, the next morning, I could walk in with confidence.

The next morning, I drove to the church. I had planned to walk in like I owned the place, but I was extremely nervous. As soon as I sat down, I heard someone behind me say, "Hey Clive, I didn't know you went to church here."

I wanted to say, "I didn't either until yesterday," but I just smiled and nodded.

The opening song was "On Holy Ground." A few months before, I bought Barbara Streisand's CD that contained her song, "On Higher Ground." She had sung "On Holy Ground" at Bill Clinton's mother's funeral, and she was inspired to make her own version of the beautiful song. *That's good,* I thought. I was starting to loosen my death grip on the seat.

That morning of all mornings, Dr. Young opened the Bible to Exodus 20 and preached a message about the Ten Commandments. (Though I was one of the few Jewish people in the room, I felt like the only one who couldn't find the passage in the pew Bible.) He explained God's greatness and purity, and he said that all of us fall far short of God's expectations. He also explained the meaning of Passover when the lamb was slain and its blood was put on the doorposts so that the Angel of Death would pass over the house. Dr. Young told about the unique role of the Jewish people to bring God's message to the world. He was talking about things that might sound odd to others in the church that morning,

"We arrive at the truth not by reason only, but also by the heart."

Blaise Pascal

but he was talking about *my* people, *my* heritage, *my* Torah, and *my* God! It was like he and I were the only two people in the room, and I hung on every word. Finally, Dr. Young explained that what was written in the Torah foretold of the Messiah who would come to fulfill prophecies and pay for the sins of the world as the ultimate Passover Lamb of God. At that moment, the heavens opened up to me, and what I intuitively felt about God suddenly rested on the truth. Centuries ago, physicist and author Blaise Pascal observed a principle that had just become true for me: "We arrive at the truth not by reason only, but also by the heart." I silently said to God, *I want to take my first step toward you!* Dr. Young gave an invitation to those who wanted to trust in Christ that morning, and I walked down front.

When I got to the front of the church, I met a man who gave me a card to fill out so I could join the church, but I gave it back to him. I said, "I don't want to join the church."

He looked puzzled. "Then why did you come down at the invitation?"

I explained simply, "Because I'm responding to Dr. Young's encouragement to raise my flag for Jesus."

We talked about the meaning of faith, and he gave me a videocassette about baptism. I went home and viewed the cassette. Carlos was in New Orleans for the weekend, but I called him on his cell. I blurted out, "Hey Carlos, I want to get baptized."

"What?" he asked incredulously. "What happened? Why do you want to do that?"

I hurriedly explained, "You'll never guess what happened." I explained the events of the past few days and that morning.

He instantly told me, "I'm coming home."

"When?"

"Right now!"

I told him that he didn't need to come back that day, and he told me he'd call me back in a few minutes. Several minutes later, Carlos called to tell me that he had a friend called Papa A who is the pastor of a church in a suburb of Houston. He said he'd baptize me in a hot tub on Monday night.

The next night, Carlos and I drove down to Papa A's. We talked for a while about my new life in Christ, and then Papa A baptized me. It was Memorial Day, May 31, 1999.

Another Change of Direction

I'm glad I'm Jewish because our tradition is painfully realistic: We expect the worst from any situation! From the time I became a Christian, everything in my life began to unravel. I had been in a relationship with a woman, but it soured and ended. The City of Houston decided it was time to dig up all the streets around the restaurant, so people had difficulty getting to us for many months, and our business declined 60%. There were other business setbacks that affected us, too. In December, I called my parents to tell them I planned to fly to New York during the Christmas holidays. I had told them about my new faith, and when we talked about plans to see them, my father told me sternly, "You're still our son. You can come home, but Clive, don't mention the name of Jesus or try to convert us." I had been through a divorce and a fire, but this was worse—much worse. If I hadn't had a new faith in the Messiah as a strong foundation, I don't know how I would have made it. I didn't blame him for any of it. He was the one who saw me through.

Actually, my trip to see my parents turned out better than I could have imagined. My father met me at the airport, but he didn't recognize me until I was about 10 feet away. He looked startled and said, "Oh, it's you! I didn't recognize you." Soon after we got to my parents' townhouse, I overheard my mother calling friends and telling them, "You've got to come over for dinner to see Clive. He's different." Those days with my family were wonderful. My relationship with my brother and sister grew much stronger. I was so much older that we hadn't been around each other very much, but now, a bond began to grow. And I was so thankful my parents recognized that a genuine change was taking place in me. According to them, I even *looked* different.

As I look back on that time, I can only guess that my family noticed the transformation God was working in my heart. In the past, I had been an angry, demanding person because I felt that I couldn't do enough to be accepted. But now I felt loved, forgiven, and completely accepted by God. Carlos had been right. When he talked to me that day after we met about placing ads for the restaurant, he had told me that I didn't have any *shalom* in my life. When I found the Messiah (or more accurately, when he found me), he began to heal my hurts and fill my life with his peace. That's what my family had seen. Today, when I tell people how angry I had been years ago, they looked shocked. Many of them tell me, "Clive,

I can't imagine you as an angry person!" I appreciate their comments more than they can know. It's evidence that God changes lives—even mine. After Moses died, God appointed Joshua to take his people into the Promised Land. He encouraged Joshua: "In the same way I was with Moses, I'll be with you. I won't give up on you; I won't leave you. Strength! Courage!" I feel like God has been saying the same thing to me since that first day with him, and it means the world to me.

From the beginning of my relationship with God, I started going to every Bible study I could attend. About two years later, I was in a study with a friend from St. Luke's Methodist Church. He needed help with a big event, and he asked if I could provide equipment and concessions. I helped him, and to thank me, he signed me up to take a personality profile, ironically called The Birkman Method. The profile analyzes more than personality traits. It also compares a person's personality to successful people in every possible career. When mine came back, the top two "Best Fit" careers for me where in the ministry. Numbers 9, 10, and 11 were in the restaurant business and hospitality. I was stunned.

On Monday, two days after I got the results of the personality profile and career assessment, one of the pastors at Second Baptist called and asked to have lunch with me. At a little Chinese restaurant, he told me, "Clive, I'm going to start a church in Tampa, Florida. Yesterday, my wife and I were praying, and we asked God who we should invite to join our pastoral staff team. Both of us sense that person is you." I was blown away! He handed me a plane ticket and told me he'd like for me to fly to Tampa to check it out over Super Bowl weekend.

I flew down to Tampa with a thousand questions. As we drove around the city and talked about what God might do there, the plans seemed to cascade from my heart onto paper. When I got back to Houston, the plan crystallized: My partner would buy out my interest in the restaurant, and I could go to seminary, open a sandwich shop to pay the bills while I was in school, serve part-time at the church, and take care of Ian's future. It seemed perfect. I believed Tampa was in God's plan for me.

A few months later, Tropical Storm Allison dropped 30 inches of rain on Houston, and our church mobilized every person to help those whose homes had been flooded. I pitched in, and I enjoyed being part of that massive effort. One day as we distributed food, Dr. Young took City Council Member Orlando Sanchez on a tour of our distribution facilities. I had known Orlando for several years. He saw me, and he walked over to greet me.

Dr. Young followed him and greeted me, too. Immediately, Orlando turned to Dr. Young and asked, "How do you know Clive Berkman?" I could almost read Orlando's mind. He was wondering, *What in the world is Clive doing working with a church? I never knew he was even interested in God.*

In June, I was asked to speak at a Saturday night event at Second Baptist. For some reason, the people at the church were seeing some potential in me. The church's program coordinator, Lisa Milne, called and asked if I'd come for a meeting with her. When we met, she asked, "Clive, do you feel called into the ministry?"

"Kind of," I replied obliquely.

She told me, "We want to offer you a six-month trial position as director of the singles ministry."

"Really?" I couldn't have been more surprised.

"Yes," she continued. "We need a director for our singles ministry, and we believe you're the right person."

I sat back in my chair and started crying. "You don't know me. I have a lot of baggage. I have a checkered background. I run a restaurant that serves wine. In fact, I teach people how to select wines. Surely, you don't want me."

Lisa smiled and shrugged as if to say, "Who cares? We want you anyway."

Instead of going to Tampa, I began my role as singles director on July 18, 2001.

Cooking and Life

"Empty bottle moments" can come at the most unexpected times and places. Actually, these times may have nothing to do with bottles, but they can be moments we'll never forget. Recently I was working on several projects at the same time, including this book. On a particular day, I had a lot that needed to be accomplished, and during the day, my stress level gradually rose near the boiling point. In addition, I caught a nasty cold. All together, I wasn't having a great day! I had scheduled an appointment in the afternoon to make progress on one of my projects, but I received a call asking me to attend an event for second graders at our church's school. Nothing, it seemed, was working out for me. Begrudgingly, I showed up at the school thinking it would be a waste of time. Over the past several months, I'd taught some classes for these kids, so many of them knew me. When I walked in, several children yelled, "Hey, Clive!" and waved to me. After their presentation, proud parents took pictures with their darling kids, and some of the children insisted that I join them in their family photos. The smiles on those kids' faces completely changed my attitude. I had thought being at their event was an interruption of my day, but it made my day! It was a moment—an empty bottle moment—I'll always remember.

Sometimes people say, "Oh, Clive. You're such a connoisseur of wine and great food." I appreciate their compliment, but I quickly tell them they are connoisseurs, too. A connoisseur is "a person competent to pass critical judgments in an art or in matters of taste," and each of us is certainly competent to determine what our families love to eat and drink. The question is: Will we do what it takes to make those meals special? For instance, I have a taste for Beluga caviar, the most expensive in the world, but a friend of mine tells me that her family loves hamburgers. Over the years, she has become an accomplished connoisseur of hamburgers! She has tried different kinds of ground beef (she prefers ground chuck for flavor and juiciness), different marinades, grilled onions, cheeses, mustards, and many other sauces and toppings. She has used grilled onion rolls, whole-wheat buns, and other types of buns. She experimented with side dishes galore, including a host of onion ring recipes as well as fresh vegetables. I asked, "Which is your family's favorite?"

She laughed, "I don't know. We love lots of different ways to cook hamburgers. And as long as I see that smile and we enjoy time together, I'm thrilled."

Some people look down their noses at people who eat hamburgers instead of chateaubriand, but that's ridiculous. Find what works, be creative, and enjoy wonderful dishes with your friends and family. Don't be a culinary snob. In my

A cooking class

dishes, I may use canned tomatoes, a package of frozen peas, whipped topping, and even (heaven forbid!) ketchup. In one of my breakfast recipes, I use ketchup, and people always tell me they love it. When they ask what's in the sauce, I tell them one of the ingredients is ketchup. The snobs look like I've just poisoned them, but the rest of the people appreciate my creativity.

Some people think they need to become experts at a particular style of cooking, and they tell me they can't cook well because they only cook "down home foods." But we can all learn to be great cooks in our own way and in our own styles. I don't really have a particular style. I try all kinds of things and take tips and techniques from everywhere. Don't feel locked into a certain school of cooking. Pick and choose the things you like, and enjoy putting things together that compliment each other.

This lesson applies to every area of life. We need to find the things that make us happy, not the things that impress others. When Ian was selecting a major in college, I told him to find something he loves to do, not what will make him the most money or propel him as a social climber. In the same way, all of us need to be humble enough to admit we like a little ketchup in our careers and hobbies, and then enjoy it to the hilt with those we love. The psalmist wrote, "What a wildly wonderful world, God! You made it all, with Wisdom at your side. You made earth overflow with your wonderful creations."

Though my role has changed over the years, I'm still in the kitchen, and I'm still learning some valuable lessons. In fact, I believe that cooking and eating with those we love teach some of life's most important lessons. Too often, we rush through an activity to get to the next one, and we rush through that one to get to the one after that. But life is about much more than speed and acquiring things. Meals offer us opportunities each day to slow down, treasure the people around us, and make them feel special. With a little care, we can create beautiful moments around the table to share hurts and hopes, fumbles and faith.

When we eat, we need to savor every morsel. Every one of our senses goes into action, and we enjoy the experience with family and friends. Rich, meaningful times over meals take a little time for preparation, presentation, and participation, but if we value people more than speed or possessions, we'll delight in showing them how much we care.

Every meal can be a time and place when we connect with people's minds and hearts, but from time to time, we go beyond this rich experience to truly celebrate each other and the important markers in our lives. As we enjoy these times together, we can leave empty bottles that tell stories of these celebrations.

I believe that recipe books are for the living room, not the kitchen. When you relax in your living room, read and be inspired to try something new. Be creative in your cooking. Try a new dish, and try different ways to prepare familiar recipes. The dish may fail. If it does, laugh and move along. But your creativity may result in something sensational that you would have never experienced if you hadn't taken a risk.

As you look at the recipes in this book, I don't want you to try to recreate the moments we enjoyed. I want you to create your own moments that you'll remember the rest of your life. I hope this book is more than a cookbook for you. It contains some wonderful recipes, but more than that, I hope you gain a new way of looking at cooking and a new perspective on life.

Even today, people ask me, "What's a nice Jewish boy like you still doing in the kitchen?" I tell them that in a sense, we're all in the kitchen because it's a symbol of life, full of joy and spills, glorious successes and burnt dishes, tender moments with and unnerving chaos. The place where masterpieces are created also produces stuff we cart off to landfills. We're all in the process of learning, growing, and laughing with each other. It's there that we develop our recipes for cooking and for life.

Making Great Memories

Maybe I'm a bit eccentric. When I started keeping empty bottles of wine at the restaurant, a few people had raised eyebrows, and a handful of intrepid souls actually asked, "Clive, what are you doing with so many empty bottles?" The people who had to clean the restaurant and dust all the surfaces each day had very strong opinions about my sanity: They thought I was crazy!

Our passion was to win Wine Spectator magazine's Grand Award, so I traveled to France and California many times each year to find the best vineyards and the best vintages for each one. We were invested heart, body, and soul in finding the best bottles of wine for our guests. With the enormous investment of time and attention in finding wines, it seems that full bottles would be our focus, but they weren't. To me, full bottles are full of potential, but they are incomplete. They have a future, but they don't tell a story yet. An empty bottle, though, tells a story about a fabulous dinner, a joyful celebration, or a night that marked a turning point in someone's life.

Empty bottles tell stories and bring back memories of good times with people. Each of the events I've held in our restaurant, in catering, and at my home was designed to create "empty bottle moments" and memories for those who came. For that to happen, we invested a lot of time coming up with creative twists so that every person would remark, "Wow! That's fantastic!" These were the signature moments for me in the restaurant business and with our guests, many of whom became my friends. We built lasting relationships with foundations and organizations, and we hosted dinners to help them raise money. All the work, though, was worthwhile, because I heard stories of lives that were forever changed. Jeff Pinkerton, a friend who worked with me on special events, often reminded me when we were both very tired, "Remember, Clive. It's for the children."

The empty bottles were meaningful to me, but they were even more meaningful to our guests. I grouped empty bottles from particular events, like the 50's night, Poodle Skirts and Flattops, or the Château Margaux dinner. The guests who had come to those events would see the bottles the next time they came to the restaurant, and they remembered the fun they had with us. The bottles also served as a reminder to wait staff of our passion and dedication to serve people so well that they'd never forget dining with us.

"We make a living by what we get;
we make a life by what we give."

Sir Winston Churchill

Memories are important to all of us. Of course, some are painful, but we shouldn't let these haunt us. We need to take more time to think about the pleasant, wonderful times we've had with family and friends. God told the children of Israel to set up piles of stones to remind them where they'd come from and where he was leading them. We didn't want to have piles of rocks in Charley's to remind people of significant events in their lives. Instead, we used empty bottles.

Sir Winston Churchill once said, "We make a living by what we get; we make a life by what we give." Empty bottles remind us of the joy in giving our hearts to others. The real meaning of life is pouring ourselves out for those we love, not in hoarding our time and our possessions for ourselves. If we try to hold things too closely, we miss life's most important moments and neglect the people who need our love. If, though, we gladly give our hearts to others, we'll share wonderful memories together. (I bet you're thinking of some right now.) Don't be in a hurry to get "one more thing" done. Slow down, enjoy people, pour your heart into them, and savor every moment—and your life will have hundreds of empty bottles, all full of wonderful memories.

When you look around your home at all the things you possess, you may realize your home is more of a full bottle of potential than an empty bottle of memories. Most of us don't really need all the stuff we've collected. We can give some of it away, perhaps anonymously, to people who really need it. Giving generously—of our time, talents, and treasure—is another way to pour out our lives and create memories we'll cherish for years. We gain much more by pouring out than by holding tightly to what we have.

I believe God delights in creating empty bottle moments for us. He gives us so many good things to enjoy and people to love. Sure, we have difficulties, but these make us appreciate God's goodness even more. God invites us to trust him to make our lives rich and full. He tells us, "Test me in this and see if I don't open up heaven itself to you and pour out blessings beyond your wildest dreams."

In these pages, I want to highlight some of the most memorable times we enjoyed. I'll share the story and give you some recipes for you to try with your family and friends, but I suggest you add your own creativity to each dish and dinner. Don't try to recreate exactly what we did—instead, create your own memorable moments.

Election Night with Mr. Bush

Tuesday, November 8, 1988 was Election Day, and candidate George Bush hoped to become the 41st president of the United States. Some of his friends in Houston, Dr. Charles and Sally Neblett, hosted a gathering in their home to watch the returns that night. The Nebletts were frequent guests at our restaurant, and they asked us to cater the dinner. For the menu, I thought it would be appropriate to prepare dishes from the states Mr. Bush would almost certainly win. The Secret Service came to the restaurant to check us out. When they were satisfied we weren't terrorists or any other kind of threat to national security, we did all of our advanced preparation.

Clive presenting the congratulatory dessert to President Bush and his wife

We arrived early at the Neblett's house to finish our preparation. Soon, the Bushes and a host of their top supporters arrived. At the time, there were only three major networks, and all the televisions in the house were tuned to those stations. Dignitaries and friends watched the news and talked about the vote, but I didn't recognize most of them because I'd only been in America a few years.

Mr. Bush sat at a piano in the living room most of the evening watching a television. At one point, I walked by him, and he called me over. Someone had told him about me, and he said, "Clive, you're an interesting person. You're Jewish from South Africa.

You studied in London and toured Europe, and you've lived in New York and Miami." For about 15 minutes, he told me about his travels and people he had met from each of the countries where I'd lived, and he added a few insights about the politics of those nations. He particularly noted the unrest over apartheid in South Africa. He told me, "Your homeland is troubled, Clive."

It was amazing. The eyes of the entire world were on him that night, but he took time to talk with me about my life.

Late that night, a man from the party came into the kitchen in a rush and told me, "The networks are just about to declare Mr. Bush the winner. Do you have anything we can give him to celebrate?"

I put three candles—red, white, and blue—in a piece of chocolate cake, and as the news anchor officially declared that he had enough electoral votes to win, I presented the cake to him with the inscription: "Congratulations, Mr. President."

A few minutes later, several photographers were taking pictures. Mr. Bush stopped them and called me over to his side. He said, "I want a picture with Clive. He was the first one to call me 'Mr. President,' and I want the picture for the White House."

THE MENU

Crabmeat and Shrimp Flan

Tortilla Soup

Blackened Texas Sirloin

Chocolate Marquis

Crabmeat and Shrimp Flan

Serves 4

2 **eggs**
1 **egg yolk**
1 cup of **half and half**
A pinch of **curry powder**
A pinch of **garlic powder**
2 ounces of **crabmeat**
4 medium (21 count) **shrimp,** shelled and cut in half
2 tablespoons of **cooked corn**
1 tablespoon of **butter**
Sea salt and **white pepper**

Whisk the eggs and yolk with garlic and curry powder. Add salt, white pepper and half and half. Mix well. Butter four 4-ounce ovenproof bowls. Place ½ ounce of crabmeat, 2 pieces of shrimp, and ½ teaspoon of corn in each bowl. Fill each bowl with the cream mixture. Place the bowls in a water bath (a roasting pan with 1 inch of water in the bottom).

Bake at 350 for 10–20 minutes.

Allow the bowls to cool for 5 minutes before serving. (You can make this dish a day in advance and reheat it in the microwave.)

Sauce

6 **peppercorns**
The zest and juice from 1 **orange**
2 ounces of **heavy cream**
2 tablespoons of **butter**

Reduce the peppercorns, the orange zest, and the juice over medium heat until 1 tablespoon is left. Add the heavy cream, and bring it to a boil. Remove it from the stove and whisk in the butter.

Strain the sauce. (If you prefer, use a sweet pepper purée instead of orange butter.) Turn each flan out on a serving plate, and spoon half a teaspoon of sauce on each plate. Garnish with extra crabmeat or corn.

Tortilla Soup

Serves 6

3 tablespoons of **olive oil**
2 **corn tortillas,** chopped
1 tablespoon of **corn oil**
1 tablespoon of **cumin powder**
½ teaspoon of **chili powder**
2 medium **onions,** finely chopped or puréed
2 **chipotle peppers,** finely chopped
2 medium **tomatoes, puréed**
1 8-ounce can of **chopped tomatoes**
2 tablespoons of **tomato paste**
3 cloves of **garlic,** chopped
4 tablespoons of chopped **cilantro**
2 **bay leaves**
2 quarts of **chicken broth**

Garnishes

4 **corn tortillas,** cut in ½ inch strips and fried in corn oil
8 ounce **chicken breast,** grilled or poached in broth and sliced into ¼ strips
1 cup of **Monterey Jack cheese**
1 medium **avocado** in small cubes
Sour cream

Heat the oil in a soup pot. When it's medium hot, add the chopped tortillas, garlic, chili powder, and cumin, and cook for 2 minutes, stirring to prevent burning.

Add onions, peppers, tomatoes, tomato paste, bay leaf, and cilantro, and bring it to a boil. Cook over medium heat, stirring until it boils. Adjust the seasoning.

Add the broth, reduce the heat, and simmer for 20–30 minutes. Add extra broth if the mixture becomes too thick.

At this point, you can strain the mixture, or you can serve it chunky without straining it. Serve in bowls. Add garnish on top, or allow your guests to choose their own.

Blackened Texas Sirloin

Serves 6

2 pounds of **New York strip sirloin,** whole
1 tablespoon of **oregano**
½ tablespoon of **cayenne pepper**
1 tablespoon of **paprika**
1 tablespoon of **garlic powder**
1 tablespoon of **crushed black pepper**
1 tablespoon of **onion powder**
1 tablespoon of **white pepper**
1 tablespoon of **salt**
1 ounce of melted **butter**

Mix all the spices together. Brush the sirloin with melted butter, and rub each side with the spice mixture. Let the steaks stand at room temperature for 30 minutes.

Heat the grill. When you're ready to cook, place the steaks on the grill over medium heat. (For more about grilling, see "Grilling and Chilling.")

Cook for 12–15 minutes (for medium-rare) turning regularly. Cook for the last 5 minutes on low/medium heat.

Remove the steaks from the heat and allow them to rest for 5 minutes.

Cut the steak into 2-ounce pieces and serve.

For sides, I recommend corn relish, cucumber salad, roasted sweet red peppers, or grilled sweet potatoes.

Chocolate Marquis

3 pounds of **bittersweet chocolate**
2 tablespoons of **Grand Marnier**
2 ounces of **espresso**
6 **egg yolks**
6 **egg whites**
1 pint of **heavy cream**

Melt the chocolate with Grand Marnier and coffee over a double boiler. (Be careful not to get any water in the mixture. That would be a major oops!) Add the yolks 1 at a time, beating well, then remove from the double boiler.

Whip the egg whites until they form soft peaks, and then fold the whites into the mixture.
Lightly whip the cream and fold it in.
Pour the mixture into a plastic-lined loaf pan and chill overnight.
Slice (⅓-inch wide) with a knife run under hot water for each slice, and serve over a crème anglaise with dots of raspberry sauce.

Broadway on the Bayou

Charley's 517 was located in the theater district in Houston, so we had many celebrities—actors, singer, playwrights, and producers—dine with us, including Carol Channing, Leslie Uggams, Marvin Hamlish, Placido Domingo, Harry Anderson, Christopher Eschenbach, and many others. From time to time, we hosted receptions in The Wine Cellar. After the show—often on opening night—the host committee, the cast, and their escorts came to the restaurant.

Clive with Carol Channing

Many artists, actors, and musicians instinctively grasp the beauty of cooking and eating together. Luciano Pavarotti said, "One of the very nicest things about life is the way we must regularly stop whatever it is we are doing and devote our attention to eating."

One of the things I learned in the restaurant business is that people, no matter what their social status, are just people. Whether their names are known around the world or if they bus tables, they have hopes and fears in life. I learned to respect each person as a valuable human being, without putting some on a pedestal and taking others for granted.

Baked Brie in Phyllo

Serve with sliced apples, pears, and sliced French bread.

Serves 8-10

¼ cup of **marmalade or apricot preserves** and 1 ounce
    of **warm water**
A 14-ounce wheel of **Brie** (whole, with no cuts or openings)
¼ cup **slivered and toasted almonds**
10 sheets of **phyllo dough**
¼ cup of **butter,** melted

Additional fillings to consider:

Walnuts	**Pecans**
Cranberry chutney	**Dried cranberries** or **cherries**

Mix the marmalade or preserves with an ounce of warm water to thin it a bit. Spread the preserves over the top of the wheel of Brie. Wrap the Brie in 2 (thawed) sheets of phyllo leaves that have been lightly brushed with butter.

Turn the cheese over, brush it lightly with melted butter, and wrap it with 2 more sheets of phyllo. Turn the cheese over again and repeat the process, using all the phyllo sheets. Cover it with a moist (but not too moist) towel and refrigerate for 1 hour (but not more than 6 hours) before cooking.

Place the Brie on a cookie sheet, and bake it at 425 for 8–10 minutes, or until the outside is golden brown. Let it stand 5 minutes before serving.

While using phyllo, always keep the unused portion covered with a lightly damp towel.

For Brie in puff pastry

Lightly flour a baking sheet, and place the puff pastry on the prepared sheet. Roll it out gently to remove the fold lines. Spread half of the marmalade onto the center of the puff pastry sheet and place the Brie on top of the marmalade. Spread the remaining marmalade over the top of the Brie. Bring the pastry up around the sides and over the cheese. Wrap it completely and trim off any excess pastry. Turn the Brie over and place the seam side down. (If you are preparing it a day ahead, cover and refrigerate it at this point. Bring it to room temperature before baking.)

Combine 1 egg and water, and brush the top. Bake at 400 for 10–12 minutes, until it's golden brown. Brush it with melted butter, and allow it to stand for 5 minutes before serving.

You can bake baby Brie or Camembert using the same recipe.

Bruschetta

Makes 24–30 pieces

1 loaf of **French bread**
2 large, ripe **tomatoes**—skinned, quartered, seeded, and finely chopped (not minced)
2 cloves of regular **garlic**, minced very fine
2 tablespoons of **balsamic vinegar**, to taste
¼ cup of **olive oil** or **butter**
4 tablespoons of **fresh basil** (be generous with the basil!)
Grated **Parmesan cheese**, as much as you like
Optional: **cream cheese** and **goat cheese**

Combine the tomatoes, balsamic vinegar, and basil, and refrigerate for several hours. Check it for taste and season accordingly. (If it's too tart, add some sugar and olive oil.)

Slice the French bread in thin pieces and sprinkle them with olive oil or butter. Bake each side until they're golden brown. Allow the bread to cool slightly, and then rub each piece with a garlic clove.

Spoon the tomato mixture onto the pieces of French bread. For extra flavor, coat the bread with an equal mixture of cream and goat cheese before adding the tomato mixture.

Sprinkle with Parmesan cheese, and serve.

Salmon Wellington

These can be made as bite-size pieces.

Serves 2

1 sheet of **puff pastry**, 8 x 10, rolled ⅛-inch thin

2 5-ounce pieces of cleaned **salmon**

2 ounces of **jumbo sea scallops**, cut in quarters and sautéed
    in butter

2 ounces of **lump crabmeat**

2 ounces of **dry sherry**

½ cup of **heavy cream**

2 tablespoons of **tarragon**

1 tablespoon of **sweet butter**

Egg wash

(You can substitute a shelled lobster tail for the salmon. Before wrapping it, sauté the tail lightly in clarified butter—don't cook it; just caramelize the outside.)

Heat the butter in a small skillet over medium heat. Sauté the scallops until they're half done, and then remove them from the pan.

To make the sauce, add the sherry, heavy cream, and tarragon, and reduce the mixture until it's the consistency of paint. Add scallops and crabmeat into the cream. Mix lightly, season, and chill.

Cut the pastry into 2 pieces, and place the filling in the center of each piece of pastry. Season the salmon fillets, and place them on top of the filling. Brush the exposed pastry with egg wash, bring the flaps over the salmon, and seal them well.

Turn the covered fish over and brush the pastry with egg wash. Allow them to rest in the refrigerator for 30 minutes before cooking.

Preheat the oven to 350 and bake for 10–12 minutes until lightly golden brown, and serve with strained sauce.

Sauce option: Soak 3 buds of saffron in 1 ounce of sherry for 15 minutes. Place the liquid in a small pot on medium heat, and reduce it by ⅓. Add 2 ounces of heavy cream, and reduce by ⅓. Season with chopped dill and sea salt.

Spinach and Artichoke Dip

Serve with fresh tortilla chips, toasted pita, or French bread.

Serves 12

2 cloves of **garlic**, minced

½ small **onion**, chopped

¼ cup of **butter**

3 tablespoons of **all-purpose flour**

2 10-ounce boxes of **frozen spinach**, thawed and squeezed dry through a colander

12-ounce jar of **artichoke hearts**, drained and coarsely chopped

2 cups of **heavy cream**

¼ cup of **sour cream**

¼ cup of **chicken broth**

⅔ cup of fresh-grated **Pecorino Romano cheese**

½ cup of shredded **white cheddar cheese**

2 teaspoons of **lemon juice**

2 tablespoons of **olive oil**

½ cup of **panko breadcrumbs**

Sea salt and **pepper**

Lightly sauté the garlic and onions in half the butter over medium heat for 3 minutes. Add the flour and the rest of the butter. Mix well, and continue to cook for 2 minutes.

Add spinach, artichokes, broth, and creams. Cook over medium heat (stirring well) for 5 minutes. Add the cheese, and season with salt, pepper, and lemon juice.

Heat 2 tablespoons of olive oil in a medium skillet over medium heat. Add 2 cloves of minced garlic, and cook them until they're lightly toasted, about 1 minute. Stir in ½ cup of panko breadcrumbs, season with sea salt, and cook another minute.

Pour the artichoke-spinach mixture in a well-buttered ceramic or Pyrex dish. Sprinkle it with crumbs, and bake at 350 for 30–40 minutes, until the crumbs turn golden brown.

Linemen Sure Can Eat!

We knew someone had made reservations for a large dinner party, but we had no idea it was this dinner party.

Months before, we had donated dinner for 20 to the Leukemia & Lymphoma Society's fundraising auction. The Houston Oilers' All-Star lineman, Mike Munchak bought the dinner. During their pre-season training, we got a call: "Reservations for 20, please." The person who took the reservation had no idea it was Mike Munchak, but the next evening, Mike walked in with 19 enormous linemen he had invited to dinner.

If we had known it was Mike's party, we would have prepared very differently. A party of 20 usually eats what 20 normal people eat, but these guys weren't normal people. Our restaurant served à la carte. They thought that term was French for "all the cart you can eat." They each ordered an appetizer and a salad—no surprises there—and they each ordered an entrée: a steak or a rack of lamb. Things went smoothly until one of the wait staff came to me and said, "These guys are ordering a second entrée, and I think they may want a third! One of them ordered châteaubriand . . . for himself!"

Our wait staff smiled and served them politely—but from then on, I secretly wanted to screen the bidders at the auction to be sure that small people got the dinner in the future.

Caesar Salad

This recipe is very close to the original version created in 1924 by Caesar Cardini, an Italian restaurateur in Tijuana, Mexico. That's right, the salad is named after its creator, a chef, not Roman emperor Julius Caesar.

Serves 4

2 medium heads of **romaine lettuce,** outer leaves removed

1 cup of **French bread,** cubed for croutons

2 cloves of **garlic**

2–3 **anchovies** (depending on your preference)

1 teaspoon of **capers**

1 teaspoon of **Worcestershire sauce**

1 teaspoon of **dry mustard**

3 tablespoons of **fresh lemon juice**

1 tablespoon of **white wine vinegar**

½ teaspoon of **freshly ground pepper**

⅓ cup of **olive oil**

A pinch of **sea salt**

⅓ cup of **Parmesan cheese**, shredded

1 **egg yolk**, at room temperature—optional (The original recipe may have called for "coddled" whole eggs that have been warmed to 120 degrees. To coddle, simmer the eggs in boiling water for 1 minute, and cool in cold water so they're soft and runny.)

Trim the romaine lettuce of bruised or browned leaves, and then cut it into 1½-inch pieces. Wash and drain the lettuce, pat it dry, and refrigerate for 30 minutes to crisp the leaves.

Peel the garlic cloves, and put them in a large, wooden salad bowl. Mash the cloves against the sides of the bowl with the back of a wooden spoon. Rub the pieces against the bowl until they begin to disintegrate. Remove most of the mashed garlic from the bowl and discard it—the oil from the garlic will remain in the bowl and flavor the salad. Add the anchovies, and repeat the procedure used with the garlic, but leave the anchovy pieces in the bowl. Now add the dry mustard, Worcestershire sauce, lemon juice, and black pepper, and blend well. Slowly drizzle in the remaining olive oil, mixing with a wire whisk. Add the egg yolk, and whisk well together. (This can be done in the food processor for a creamier consistency.)

Add the lettuce, croutons, Parmesan cheese, and salt. Mix it together, and serve directly from the salad bowl.

Croutons

To make croutons, cut the bread into ½-inch cubes, heat ½ cup of olive oil in a sauté pan over medium-high heat. Fry the bread cubes in the oil, tossing frequently, until they're crisp and golden. Season the hot croutons with 2 tablespoons of Parmesan cheese, salt, and paprika. Reserve the croutons until you're ready to use them.

Corn Chowder

Serves 4-6

2 **bacon rashers,** cut into pieces
2 tablespoons of **olive oil**
2 small **yellow onions**, chopped
½ cup of **celery**, chopped
2 large **potatoes**, cubed and cooked tender in boiling salted water
4 ears of **corn**, roasted on a grill and cut off the cob
2 tablespoons of **all-purpose flour**
6 cups of **chicken broth**
2 cups of **light white wine** (Sauvignon Blanc or Chenin Blanc) reduced by half
2 cups of **heavy cream**
Salt, **pepper**, and **cayenne pepper** to taste

Sauté the bacon in the olive oil for 2 minutes over medium heat. Add celery and onion, and cook until they are translucent.

Add potatoes and corn, and season with salt and cayenne pepper. Mix in the flour, and cook together for 2–3 minutes, stirring often. Add warm stock slowly, and simmer (on low) for 10 minutes. Add cream, and cook for an additional 10 minutes.

Adjust the seasoning, and serve, garnished with chopped, roasted peppers or oven-roasted tomatoes.

You also can make this with smoked salmon or trout, substituting fish stock or clam broth for the chicken broth. Add 4 ounces of chopped, smoked seafood with the cream.

Steak Diane

In Greek mythology, Diana was the goddess of the hunt. Traditionally, this dish used venison. Steak Diane is a classic meat dish. To properly be served, it must be prepared at tableside, which is a great way to impress your guests.

Serves 2

4 (3 ounces each) **center-cut, beef tenderloin medallions,** trimmed
4 tablespoons of **butter,** divided
Salt and pepper to taste
2 tablespoons of **shallots or green onions,** finely chopped
⅛ teaspoon of **garlic,** minced
¼ cup of **mushroom caps,** sliced ⅛-inch thick
1 teaspoon of **Worcestershire sauce**
1 teaspoon of **Dijon mustard**
¼ teaspoon of **fresh thyme leaves**
¼ cup of **heavy cream**
1 ounce (2 tablespoons) of **brandy or cognac**
1 tablespoon of fresh **parsley leaves,** chopped
1 tablespoon of **fresh chives,** chopped
½ teaspoon of **salt** (or to taste)
Coarsely ground **black pepper** to taste

Working with one piece of steak at a time, place each one between two pieces of plastic wrap. Working from the center to the edges, gently pound each piece of steak with a meat mallet to ½-inch thick.

In a small frying pan (8- or 10-inch) over medium heat, heat 1 tablespoon of butter for 1 minute. Season with salt and pepper, and add the tenderloin steaks to the pan, increase the heat to medium-high, and sauté exactly 2 minutes on each side. Remove them to a plate to rest for 5 minutes. (If you're making this dish in advance, chill the steaks at this point.)

In a large frying pan over medium heat, melt the remaining 3 tablespoons of butter. Add the shallots or green onions, garlic, and mushrooms in the center of the pan, and sauté for 2 minutes. Add the Worcestershire sauce, mustard, and thyme, and cook for 1 minute. Add the heavy cream, and bring the mixture to a boil. Check for seasoning.

Place the tenderloin steaks in the pan, and cook them to the desired doneness.

Leave the steaks in the pan, and add the brandy (or cognac) into the front edge of the pan. Turn the heat to high, and let the flame catch the brandy's vapors to ignite it. Swirl slightly, turn off the heat, and let the flame go out. (Be careful not to add the brandy directly over the flame or it could ignite the whole bottle!)

Place the steak medallions on individual serving plates, and top them with the sauce from the pan. Sprinkle with chopped parsley and chives.

Note: You may want to slightly undercook the steaks prior to adding the cream and brandy so that the reduction process of making the sauce doesn't overcook them.

Caramel Pecan Apple Crisp

Serve with vanilla ice cream or whipped cream.

Serves 6

Filling

6 medium **Granny Smith apples,** peeled, cored, and sliced ¼-inch thick (about 7 cups)
¼ cup of **sugar**
3 tablespoons of **all-purpose flour**
1½ teaspoons of **cinnamon**
2 teaspoons of **lemon juice**

Topping

1 **large egg,** separated
¼ cup of **light brown sugar**
1 stick of **butter,** ice cold, cut into 8 pieces
¾ cup of **all-purpose flour**
3 tablespoons of **pecans,** coarsely chopped

Preheat the oven to 375.

Grease a 9-inch round pie dish.

Place the apples in a large bowl, and toss them with the sugar, flour, cinnamon, and lemon juice until the slices are well coated. Mound the apples high on the pie plate.

For the topping, put the egg white into a small dish and froth it with a fork. Set it aside.

Put the egg yolk, along with the remaining ingredients (except for the pecans) in a food processor. Using a metal blade, pulse the topping until it's finely crumbed and just beginning to clump together (be careful not to overdo it).

Distribute the topping evenly over the apples, pat it to cover them completely, and press it down so that the topping sticks. Brush it with some egg white.

Scatter the pecans over the top, gently press them into the crust, and brush with more egg white.

Place the pie plate on the cookie sheet and bake for 45–50 minutes, until the top is dark brown.

Allow the dish to cool on a wire rack for at least 1½ hours before serving. Just before serving, reheat it in a 350-degree oven for about 10 minutes.

4gers in Town

The Astrodome in Houston

When the Oilers played at home, owners, coaches, and players of the visiting teams often came to our restaurant. One year when the San Francisco 49ers played in Houston, owner Eddie DeBartolo's son brought 24 of his staff to dine with us the night before the game. I met with them and recommended some dishes with a Texas flavor, and one of the staff gave me two tickets to the game. I graciously accepted, but I already had a pair of tickets.

I decided to give the tickets away the next day before the game. I stood on the sidewalk at the Astrodome near some scalpers. As a man walked up, the scalper offered him two tickets for $50. I offered him my tickets for free. The man looked surprised and pleased, and he quickly took the tickets out of my hand. The scalper wasn't quite so pleased! At that moment, I heard the gruff voice of someone behind me saying, "You two. Come with me." It was a policeman arresting scalpers. I tried to explain that I had given my tickets away, but he wasn't buying my story. He asked for my ID, but I had left my wallet at home. I had no identification. The officer looked me over and said, "You have a funny accent. Where are you from?"

I explained that I was from South Africa, but I'd lived in Houston for several years. The officer didn't believe me, so he began booking me. The scalper was a large African American, and when he heard that I was from South Africa, he became furious and threatened me. At the time, apartheid was being overturned in my homeland, and African Americans saw white South Africans as oppressors.

The officer realized I was in danger, so he quickly wrote me a ticket and let me go. Eventually, I proved my identity and got the ticket rescinded, but it was a harrowing experience. All I had done was give football tickets away, but as the saying goes: No good deed goes unpunished.

Blackened Shrimp Quesadillas

Quesadillas are toasted tortillas with melted cheese inside. In addition to cheese, you can put practically anything in them. For the 49ers staff, we made quesadillas with blackened shrimp and served them with mango salsa.

Serves 4

Flour tortillas (6-inch)
Grated cheese—either mild or sharp cheddar, Monterey Jack, or Mozzarella. You can mix in a little goat cheese for extra flavor.

You might want to add:

Grilled shrimp cut in small pieces
Caramelized red onions
Avocado
Mango salsa
Smoked salmon
Grilled chicken
Roasted garlic
Chopped tomatoes
Grilled asparagus
Chopped cilantro or basil
Black beans
Cooked spinach

Lay the tortillas flat on the counter, and sprinkle or spread the cheese on one half of each one. Add any extra ingredients—but not too thick. Then add more cheese on top and fold the tortillas in half—or you can make them round and use 2 tortillas for each quesadilla.

In a cast-iron (or thick-bottomed) skillet, add clarified butter (enough to coat the bottom). Heat the butter over medium heat, and add the quesadillas—don't crowd the skillet. Cook them on each side 1–2 minutes, until they are lightly golden brown. Remove the quesadillas from the heat, and allow them to cool 2 minutes. Slice in wedges.

Serve with sour cream or pico de gallo.

See "Grilling and Chilling" for the recipe for fresh pico de gallo.

Red Pepper Soup

Serves 6

6 large, perfect **red bell peppers**
4 tablespoons of **butter**
2 **onions**, finely chopped
3 cups of **chicken stock**
Salt and **pepper**
2 teaspoons of **vinegar**
12 **fresh basil leaves**, cut crosswise into thin strips (or you
    can substitute marjoram, cilantro, or oregano)
½ cup of **crème fraiche** (recipe found on page 111)

Remove all the stems and seeds from the peppers, and cut them into fairly small pieces. Heat the butter, and sauté the onions for 3–4 minutes, until they are translucent. Add the cut-up peppers and the chicken stock. Simmer slowly, uncovered for about 15 minutes, until the peppers are tender but still brightly colored.

Season with salt and pepper and a touch of vinegar.

Purée the soup in a food processor, and chill overnight to allow the flavor to develop fully.

Serve in small bowls, each garnished with shredded fresh herbs and a small spoonful of crème fraiche.

THE MENU

Blackened Shrimp
Quesadillas

Red Pepper Soup

Grilled Duckling and
Spiced Pecan Salad

Kathleen's Pralines

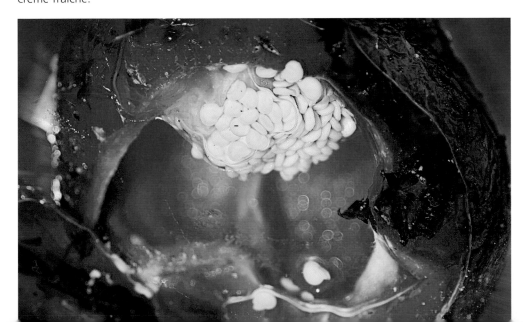

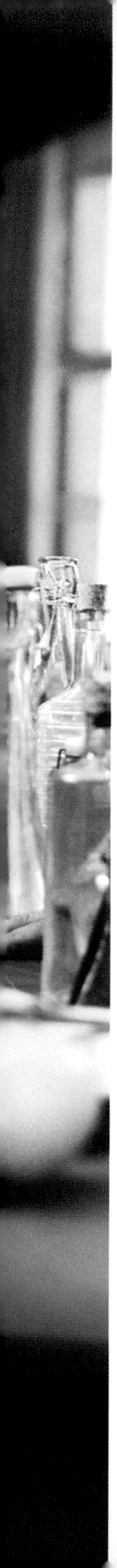

Grilled Duckling and Spiced Pecan Salad

Serves 4–6

2 pounds of **duck breast**, boned and trimmed
¼ cup of **soy sauce**
2 tablespoons of **honey**
1½ teaspoons of **sesame oil**
2 tablespoons of **dry sherry**
2 garlic **cloves**, chopped
1 tablespoon of grated **ginger**

Spiced Pecans

1½ teaspoons of **butter**
1 teaspoon of **hot chili oil**
1 cup of **pecan halves**
¼ teaspoon of **sea salt**

Cranberries

1 cup of **cranberries**
1 cup of **water**
½ cup of **sugar**

Salad and Dressing

1 ounce of **balsamic vinegar**
4 ounces of **light olive oil**
¼ teaspoon of **sea salt**
Fresh ground pepper
6 cups of **mixed salad greens**

Score each piece of the duck breast by making crosswise cuts ½ inch apart through the skin and part of the fat. Combine the soy sauce, honey, sesame oil, sherry, garlic, and ginger. Marinate the duck for 1 hour in the refrigerator, then 1 hour at room temperature.

Preheat the oven to 350. Line a baking sheet with kitchen parchment. To prepare the spiced pecans, combine the butter and chili oil, and heat them in a 9-inch skillet over moderate heat. Add the pecans and salt, stirring briefly until the liquid has evaporated.

Transfer the nuts to the baking sheet and bake them for 10 minutes, until the oil sheen has almost disappeared. Allow them to cool.

Combine the cranberries with the water and sugar in a small saucepan. Bring the water to a simmer, and when the first berry splits its skin, remove the pan from the heat and drain. Cool and reserve the berries.

Heat a heavy skillet, and when it's moderately hot, add duck breasts fat side down. Cook 4–5 minutes, moving often—it will darken and caramelize. Turn the breasts and cook the other side for about 2–3 minutes, until they are medium-rare. Let them rest 5 minutes, then remove them from the pan. Just before serving, slice the duck breasts in thin long strips across the grain.

Whisk together the ingredients for the dressing, and add the greens. Place the salad onto individual plates, and arrange the strips of duck on top. Sprinkle the cranberries and spiced pecans on top of each salad and serve immediately.

Garnish each dish with ¼ cup of fresh cranberries.

Kathleen's Pralines

Kathleen is the wife of the original owner of Charley's 517.

Serves 4

1 tablespoon of **butter**
2 tablespoons of **brown sugar**
4 tablespoons of **pecan pieces**
2 ounces of **orange juice**
A pinch or two of **cinnamon**
2 ounces of **Chambord** (raspberry liqueur)

Melt the butter in a saucepan, and then add the brown sugar. Cook over medium heat until it's lightly caramelized. Add the pecans and orange juice, and cook for 3 more minutes.

Add in Chambord (it may flame if you're using a gas stovetop), and sprinkle with cinnamon. If the mixture becomes too thick, add a little more orange juice. The consistency should be like syrup.

Pour it over dishes of vanilla ice cream.

The syrup may be prepared ahead of time and reheated before serving.

Oil Barrels and Stock Markets

In the mid-80's, the oil market collapsed, and the price of oil plummeted near $10 a barrel. Houston's economy floated on oil, and when the price went that low, the entire economy collapsed. Businesses closed, and people who couldn't pay their mortgages and couldn't sell their homes simply packed up moved away, leaving their homes empty. Our lunch business consisted primarily of businessmen with expense accounts, and during this time, company accountants scaled back spending in every possible way. People were staying away from fine restaurants in droves!

To bring business back, we decided to have the "Oil Barrel Special." We priced our lunch menu at the daily price of a barrel of oil, and we posted the price outside the restaurant to bring attention to our promotion. I'm not sure if people thought the lunch deal was exceptional or they realized we were all in this together, but whatever the reason, many of them returned to have lunch with us.

At another time, we tied the price of lunch to the stock market close the previous day. In a newspaper article in September 2002, Shelby Hodge explained, "At last, a reason to celebrate the market going down (other than selling short). Beginning today, Charley's 517 is basing the price of its 'Wall Street Special' on stock market levels of the previous day. For example, if Nasdaq closes at 1375 on Monday, the dinner special on Tuesday will be $13.75. Say the Dow Jones closes at 8400, cost of the lunch special the following day would be $8.40. Bon appetit."

Bon appetit, indeed!

Curried Chicken Salad

Perfect for a summer buffet

Serves 6-8

The chicken

3 pounds of **chicken breasts**, boned and skinned
1 **onion**, halved
1 **bay leaf**
4 sprigs of **parsley**
½ teaspoon of **salt**
¼ teaspoon of fresh **ground black pepper**
1 **clove**

Combine the chicken breasts and the onion in a saucepan. Cover them with cold water and bring it to a boil. Add the bay leaf, parsley, salt, pepper, and clove, and then simmer for 12-15 minutes, until the chicken is done. Transfer the chicken to a strainer until it's cool enough to handle.

Cut the chicken breasts into 1-inch squares or bite-sized slices.

The salad

1 cup of **water chestnuts**, sliced (fresh or canned)
½ cup of **scallions**, cut diagonally
Optional:
The grated rind of 2 **limes**
1 **cantaloupe**, cut with a melon baller
Grapes
Walnuts

Place the chicken in a bowl, and add water chestnuts, scallions, and any optional items you prefer. Mix gently.

The dressing

1 cup of **mayonnaise**
2 tablespoons of **soy sauce**
¼-⅓ cup of **curry powder**
1 cup of **mango chutney**, finely chopped

Mix the dressing ingredients, and pour it over the chicken. Toss gently.

Condiments and garnishes

1 **unsweetened coconut**, grated
2 **bananas**, peeled, sliced, and sprinkled with lemon juice
1 **mango**, peeled and diced into ½-inch cubes
½ cup of **seedless raisins**
½ cup of shelled **green peas**, boiled for 3 minutes
1 large **tomato**, diced together with ½ red onion
1 **red** and 1 **yellow pepper**, sliced
½ cup of **mango chutney**
Poppadoms
Radicchio
Arrugula
Chives, cut in ½-inch sticks

Serve the salad with these condiments and garnishes arranged around the chicken platter.

RECIPES

Curried Chicken Salad

Spinach Enchiladas

Chicken Fried Tenderloin

Red Beans and Rice

Spinach Enchiladas

Serves 4–6

1 package of **flour tortillas** (10–12 count)
¼ cup of sliced **green onions** (white ends only)
1 tablespoon of **butter**
1 10-ounce package of **frozen spinach**, thawed and drained
1 cup of **ricotta cheese**
½ cup of **sour cream**
2 cups of shredded **Monterrey Jack cheese**
1 10-ounce can of **enchilada sauce**
More **sour cream** and sliced **green onions**

    Preheat the oven to 375. In a medium saucepan, sauté the onions in butter until they are tender. Add the spinach, and cook the mixture until all the moisture has evaporated. Remove the pan from the heat. Stir in the ricotta, sour cream, and 1 cup of cheese.

    Bring the tortillas to room temperature. Spoon ½ cup of the mixture in each tortilla, and roll it up. Place these in a 13 x 9 pan, and pour the sauce over them. Add more cheese and onions on top, and bake for 15–20 minutes.

Chicken Fried Tenderloin

Serves 4

1½ pound of **beef tenderloin**
2 cups of **all-purpose flour**
½ teaspoon of **garlic powder**
½ teaspoon of **paprika**
½ teaspoon of **sea salt**
½ teaspoon of **lemon pepper**
¼ teaspoon of **cayenne pepper**
½ cup of **whole milk**
½ cup of **buttermilk**
Vegetable oil
Black pepper to taste

Cut the tenderloin into 4 equal pieces, and pound each one between pieces of wax paper to tenderize them.

Mix the flour and seasonings in a pie plate. Mix the whole milk and buttermilk in a second pie plate. Coat the tenderloin on all sides in the flour mixture, then dip it in the milk mixture, and dip it again in flour to coat all the sides.

Set the pieces of tenderloin aside on wax paper for 10 minutes to allow the coating to set.

In large frying pan, heat enough oil to cover the bottom of the pan and up the sides ¼–½ inch. Heat the oil over medium heat until the oil shimmers. Carefully slide the coated pieces of meat into the hot oil and fry them until the tenderloin is browned on each side. Cook to desired doneness—medium-rare to medium is recommended. Don't allow the meat to touch the side of pan because the batter may stick and break away. Put the cooked meat on a serving plate.

Drain off the excess oil, but keep about ½ cup of drippings. Add enough flour to the drippings to form a thick paste. Cook this over medium-low heat for 3 minutes, adding milk until the desired thickness is reached. Use a wire whisk to prevent lumps. The gravy thickens as it boils. Salt and pepper to taste.

Serve with mashed potatoes.

Red Beans and Rice

Serves 8

2 pounds of **red kidney beans**, dry
1 large **onion**, chopped
1 **red bell pepper**, chopped
4 ribs of **celery**, chopped
As much **garlic** as you like, 4–5 cloves, minced
1 large **smoked ham hock** or ¾ pound of **Creole-seasoned meat**
1–1½ pounds of **mild or hot smoked sausage or andouille**, sliced on the bias
½–1 teaspoon of dried **thyme leaves**, crushed
1 or 2 **bay leaves**
As many dashes of **Crystal hot sauce** or **Tabasco** as you like
A few dashes of **Worcestershire sauce**
Creole seasoning blend, to taste or **red pepper** and **black pepper** to taste
Salt to taste
Fresh Creole hot sausage or chaurice, links or patties, grilled or pan-fried, one link or patty
per person (optional)
Pickled onions (optional)

Soak the beans overnight if possible. The next day, drain them and put fresh water in the pot. (This helps reduce the, um, flatulence factor.) Bring the beans to a rolling boil. Make sure the beans are always covered by water or they'll discolor and get hard. Boil the beans for 45–60 minutes, until they are tender but not falling apart, then drain off the liquid.

While the beans are boiling, sauté the Trinity of Creole food—onions, celery, and bell pepper—until the onions turn translucent. Add the garlic and sauté for 2 more minutes, stirring occasionally. After the beans are boiled and drained, add the sautéed vegetables, then add the ham hock, smoked sausage, seasonings, and enough water to cover it.

Bring the pot to a boil, and then reduce the heat to a low simmer. Cook for 2 hours at least, preferably 3, until the mixture gets nice and creamy. Adjust the seasonings as you go. Stir occasionally, making sure that it doesn't burn or stick to the bottom of the pot. (If the beans are old—older than six months to a year—they won't get creamy, so make sure the beans are reasonably fresh. If it's still not getting creamy, take 1 or 2 cups of beans out and mash them, then return them to the pot and stir.)

If you can, let the beans cool, stick them in the fridge, and reheat and serve them for dinner the next day. They'll taste a lot better! You'll need to add a little water to get them to the right consistency.

Serve generous ladles of beans over hot, white long-grain rice, with good French bread. I also love to serve fresh Creole hot sausage or chaurice (grilled or broiled) on the side.

Chicken Soup for the Trophy

Temple Emmanuel hosted a competition to honor the best chicken soup in the city. I'm sure they thought nice Jewish mothers and grandmothers would be the only people to enter, but a nice Jewish boy decided to enter, too. I won it two years in a row.

One of the years I won, the Houston Chronicle wrote a feature article about my soup and me. The article appeared next to a picture of Rockets' coach Rudy Tomjanovich, whose team was surging to the playoffs. (I'm not much of a basketball player, but I'd bet I could beat him in a contest to cook chicken soup.) The article by Claudia Feldman appeared in January 1995. She described the competition: "For hard-core soup lovers, the challenge was awesome. A few brave souls (this reporter included) tried all 24 soups, but they emerged from the gantlet with hanging bellies, scorched tongues and soup dribbling down their chins. Others elected to be more discriminating, stopping after seven or eight samples. One woman danced in and out of the aisles casting a shrewd eye on the simmering pots. The chef from Charley's 517, she observed, had 'floaters.' She didn't mean dead bodies or funny things darting across eyeballs but light and fluffy matzo balls."

My recipe, of course, was one my grandmother had passed down to me. During the competition, Feldman interviewed me, and she reported two of my secrets: "When making the matzo meal concoction, [Berkman] says, whip the eggs. They need to be airy. And when you're ready to form the matzo balls, he says, the less handling the better. Says Berkman, 'One, two, three, roll.'"

My grandmother would be proud. Soup can be the highlight of any meal, not to mention a meal in itself.

First Prize Chicken Soup

Serves 6–8

Stock

5–6 pounds of **chicken bones**, including necks and feet, coarsely chopped
1 medium **carrot**, peeled, trimmed, and cut into 1-inch slices
1 medium **onion**, peeled, trimmed, and quartered
1 small **celery stalk**, trimmed, and cut into 1-inch slices
3 sprigs **fresh parsley** with stems
1 **bay leaf**
8 **whole white peppercorns**

Soup

1 whole **chicken** and 12 wings
Salt and **pepper**
3 large **carrots**, cut into small cubes
2 large **onions**, cut into small cubes
3 **celery stalks**, cut into small cubes
3 **whole cloves**
Matzo balls, made from a mix
2 tablespoons of **fresh parsley**, chopped
1 **carrot**, sliced and cooked in soup broth

Place the chicken bones in a 6- or 7-quart pot, add enough cold water to cover them, and bring it to a rolling boil. Skim off the foam and fat that collects on the top.

Add the remaining ingredients for the stock, lower the heat to a simmer, and simmer uncovered for 2–3 hours, skimming as necessary. Strain the stock through a fine-mesh strainer into a clean bowl, and let it cool. (The stock can be made a few days in advance. If you refrigerate it, discard the hardened layer of fat before using the stock in the soup.)

Add the chicken, wings, vegetables, and cloves to the stock. Skim foam off the top when it starts boiling, and cook it at a medium boil for an additional hour. Strain the soup. Remove the chicken and take the meat off the bone, cutting it into small pieces. Add the meat back to the soup, and garnish with parsley and carrots.

While the soup is cooking, prepare the matzo balls according to package directions, and cook them in salted water. When they're done, set them aside.

Ladle the soup evenly onto 6 to 8 bowls, and add 1 or 2 matzo balls to each bowl.

Curried Butternut Squash Soup

Serves 8-10

4 tablespoons of **sweet butter**
2 cups of chopped **yellow onions**
1 (and up to 3, depending on your taste) tablespoons of
    curry powder
2 medium **butternut squash** (approximately 3 pounds)
2 **apples**, peeled and chopped
3 cups of **chicken broth** (without MSG)
1 cup of **apple juice**
Salt and **pepper** to taste
½ cup of **heavy cream** (optional)

    In a saucepan, cook the onion in 1 tablespoon of the butter over moderately low heat until it's softened. Add the salt and curry powder, and cook for 3 minutes, stirring often.

    Add the squash and apple. Cover and cook the mixture over low heat for 10–15 minutes, until the squash is tender.

    Add the stock and simmer for 15 minutes. You may want to add ½ cup of heavy cream and bring the mixture to a boil.

    In a small saucepan, cook the remaining 3 tablespoons of butter over moderate heat until it is nut-brown, and add it to the stock mixture. Allow it to cool down for 10 minutes.

    In a blender or food processor, purée the mixture in batches and strain it through a fine sieve. Salt and pepper to taste.

    Serve in bowls, and garnished with your choice of blue cheese, walnuts, freshly chopped sage, or parsley.

    This soup can be made a day in advance.

RECIPES

First Prize Chicken Soup

Curried Butternut Squash Soup

Gazpacho

Croutons

Chilled Cucumber Soup

Cauliflower Vichyssoise

Tomato Basil Soup

Parmesan Twists

Gazpacho

The origin of the word gazpacho is uncertain, but etymologists believe it might be derived from the Mozarab word *caspa*, meaning "residue" or "fragments." This delicious soup is best when made in the height of the tomato season. The key is that the vegetables are chopped very finely.

Serves 8

1 cup of ripe **tomatoes**, chopped, peeled, and seeded
1 **sweet red pepper**, finely chopped
3 ribs of **celery**, finely chopped
1 **English hothouse cucumber,** finely chopped
1 small **sweet onion**, finely chopped
2 teaspoons of **parsley**, chopped
2 teaspoons of **chives**, chopped
1 clove of **garlic,** minced
2 tablespoons of **tarragon wine vinegar**
2 tablespoons of **olive oil**
1 teaspoon of **salt**
¼ teaspoon of **freshly ground pepper**
2 cups of **V8 juice**

Gazpacho is traditionally made in a mortar. The bread used to prepare this soup is ideal when it's about a week old. The bread and vegetable mixture is pounded to a paste, and then you gradually add the tomatoes, then the olive oil, and finally the vinegar, tasting all the time to make sure you've got it right. The tomatoes should always go through a sieve so there are no seeds in the finished dish.

Combine all the ingredients, and chill for 8 hours. Garnish with 1 cup of croutons (and possibly, grilled shrimp), and serve well-chilled.

Croutons

1 large loaf of **French bread**, not sliced
2 cubes of **butter**
2 tablespoons of **olive oil**
2 cloves of **garlic**, finley minced
Parmesan cheese
A blend of **paprika, garlic powder**, and **sea salt** (equal parts)

Cut the bread in approximately ½-inch cubes. Melt the butter, olive oil, and garlic together. Toss the bread cubes in the butter mixture. Put a single layer of bread cubes on a large cookie sheet, and sprinkle the season mixture to your taste. Bake in a 350-degree oven for ½ hour. Watch them closely—you may want to take them out and turn them with spatula halfway through baking. Remove the croutons from the oven and sprinkle them with Parmesan cheese while they're still hot.

Chilled Cucumber Soup

Serves 2–3

2 **English hothouse cucumbers**, ¾ peeled and seeded
1 clove of **garlic,** minced
⅔ cup of **sour cream**
1 cup (8 ounces) of **plain yogurt**
2 tablespoons of **fresh dill**
1 tablespoon of **walnuts**, chopped
Salt and **pepper**

Put the cucumbers, garlic, sour cream, and yogurt in a food processor, and blend until smooth. Add the dill, mix well, and chill.
When you are ready to serve, check the seasoning. Garnish with dill and toasted walnuts.

Cauliflower Vichyssoise

Serves 6–8

2 ounces of **butter** (more if needed)
2 **leeks** (white parts only), cut in small pieces
3 **garlic** cloves, chopped
1 medium **potato**, sliced
2 small heads of **cauliflower**, broken into small florets (reserve a small amount for the topping)
6 cups of **chicken broth**
Salt and **pepper**
4 ounces of **heavy cream** (optional)
½ cup of **chopped chives**

Melt the butter in a thick-bottomed pot (Le Creuset is best). Add leeks and garlic, and cook over medium heat for 2–3 minutes, until they are soft, stirring often. Add potatoes and continue to cook for 5 minutes (don't allow anything to brown). Cover with a lid during this time and stir every minute.

Add cauliflower and 6 cups of broth to the pot, and simmer for 20–30 minutes. Purée the soup in an immersion blender—add more stock if needed after the soup is puréed.

Cool and adjust the seasoning, and add cream if you desire.

Serve with a sprinkling of the reserved cauliflower (roasted) and the chopped chives.

To roast cauliflower, lightly coat the florets with olive oil, season with salt, pepper, sugar, and a pinch of turmeric. Bake in a 400-degree oven until they are tender.

Tomato Basil Soup

The favorite of cold soups

Serves 8

3 tablespoons of **sweet butter** or **light olive oil**
1 **sweet onion**, chopped
4 ripe **tomatoes**, peeled and chopped (no seeds)
1 14-ounce can of **whole or diced tomatoes**
1½ cups of **chicken stock**
12 **fresh basil leaves**
½ cup of **heavy cream**
Salt and **cracked black pepper** to taste

Melt the butter in a saucepan, and add the onions. Cook slowly for 3–4 minutes. Add the tomatoes, juice, and/or stock into the saucepan, and simmer 30 minutes. Add the basil leaves, and purée the mixture in small batches in a blender or food processor.

Return the mixture to the saucepan and add cream, stirring constantly over low heat.

Garnish with shredded basil leaves, or perhaps, small croutons, shrimp, or crème fraiche.

Parmesan Twists

The perfect accompaniment for soups

Serves 12

1 pound of **puff pastry**
¾ cup of **Parmesan cheese**, grated
Sweet paprika
Egg wash

Roll out the puff pastry dough into a rectangle 20 X 24 inches. Sprinkle half of the Parmesan evenly over the dough, and gently press the cheese into the dough with the rolling pin. Sprinkle with paprika. Fold the dough in half crosswise, roll it out again to 20 by 24 inches, and sprinkle on the remaining cheese.

Using a sharp, thin knife, cut the dough into ⅓-inch strips. Take each strip by its end, and twist until it is evenly corkscrewed. Lay the twists of dough on an ungreased baking sheet, arranged so they are just touching each other to keep them from untwisting. Brush lightly with egg wash.

Set the baking sheet in the middle of a preheated 350-degree oven, and bake for 15–20 minutes until the twists are crisp, puffed, and brown.

Remove the twists from the oven, cool them for 5 minutes, and then cut them apart with a sharp knife. Finish cooling the straws on a rack, and then store them in an airtight tin or a plastic bag until serving time.

The twists can be frozen.

True Concessions

I've always enjoyed outdoor entertaining. When I was just a boy, I organized fetes (mini carnivals) a few Saturdays each year. I made or bought little toys as prizes for the games I set up, such as having children catch "fish" that may or may not get them a prize. Each child got a fishing rod that had a magnet dangling from the line, and a school of paper fish swam in a blue-painted "pond" in our front yard. We had many other games, too. Children could throw darts at balloons, and some of the balloons had little pieces of paper that got them a prize. As I got older, I let children shoot my BB gun at the balloons instead of throwing darts (but my parents quickly banned that version of the game). Another popular game was throwing rings onto bottles. We spent many hours of fun at these fetes.

The games were only part of the fun. I made fresh lemonade and cooked little hamburgers for my guests. We had a marvelous time!

Many years later, my passion for fetes was resurrected when a friend asked me to participate in Houston's 4th of July Festival. I came up with a novel idea of putting shrimp on quesadillas. They were delicious, but I'm afraid my idea was ahead of its time. Hardly anybody bought them, and our booth was a colossal failure.

A couple of years later, another friend asked me to participate in The Great Tastes of Houston. Even though my quesadillas hadn't been a big hit, I wasn't going to take turkey legs, sausage-on-a-stick, or funnel cakes to the festival. I cooked crab cakes with shoestring potatoes, and we won the prize for the best food that year. Later, this became one of our most popular items at the restaurant.

Success at Great Tastes of Houston propelled me to start a new venture, True Concessions. Later, the Houston International Festival invited us to cook for their featured booth. Each year, the steering committee picked a country to feature. We studied the foods and drink indigenous to the country, and we cooked special dishes for people to enjoy. Our success at the festival encouraged us to expand our operation. We also had one of the most popular booths at the Houston Livestock Show and Rodeo. The schedule at the rodeo was grueling. It took us a week to set up, we cooked and served every day for three weeks, and then it took us a month to recuperate—but I loved it. We served standard rodeo fare: stuffed baked potatoes, but we also introduced chicken fried steak sandwiches and ribeye sandwiches. One year, we tried crab cakes and shrimp fritters, but rodeo people didn't go for something so sophisticated. They'd rather have meat and potatoes.

We served at the laser light show, The Power of Houston, and we had the concessions at the Miller Outdoor Theater, the Alley Theater, Lollapalooza, and even Whoop It Up, a 3 on 3 basketball tournament. The local newspaper sometimes heard that we were doing something special in our catering. At one point they reported, "Don't look for Charley's 517 managing director Clive Berkman this holiday weekend. He's at the United States Embassy in Bogotá, Colombia, preparing Texas barbecue for 500 Colombian VIPs, quite a departure from the usual bill of fare for his catering arm here, Crème de la Crème."

I love to do catering and concessions in a festival atmosphere—and it all started in my front yard when I was a boy in South Africa.

Shrimp Fritters

Makes approximately 20 fritters

2 **eggs**, lightly beaten
¾ cup of **milk**
1¼ cups of **all-purpose flour**
2½ tablespoons of **baking powder**
¾ teaspoon of **salt**
1¼ teaspoons of **minced red onion**
1 **Serrano pepper**, seeded and chopped
3 tablespoons of diced, mixed **sweet peppers**
6 tablespoons of **dark beer**, preferably an ale
1¼ pounds of chopped **raw shrimp** (26 count)

Beat the eggs with the milk in a large bowl. Add the flour, baking powder, salt, vegetables, and beer, and mix thoroughly.

Fold in the shrimp, and set it aside in the refrigerator to rest for 1 hour.

After you take it out of the refrigerator, adjust consistency with flour or beer.

Heat the oil in a deep frying pan to 350 degrees, and drop tablespoons full of the fritter batter into the hot oil. (Don't overfill the pan. I prefer doing 4 at a time.) Cook them for about 3–4 minutes, until they're golden brown, turning the fritters from time to time to ensure even cooking. Remove the fritters from the oil and drain them on paper towels.

Serve with a wedge of lime.

You can use mango salsa or coleslaw as a side accompaniment.

RECIPES

Shrimp Fritters

Bahamian Lamb Curry

Babootie

Lemon-Herb Marinated
Roast Chicken

Aruban Bread Pudding
with Rum Sauce

Bahamian Lamb Curry

Serves 6

¼ cup of **vegetable oil**
2 pounds of **boneless lamb shoulder or leg,** cut in 1-inch cubes
2 tablespoons of **butter**
1 cup of finely chopped **onion**
½ cup of finely chopped **celery**
3 cloves of minced **garlic**
1–2 tablespoons of **curry powder**
1 tablespoon of **tomato paste**
1 quart of **chicken broth**
1 teaspoon of **fresh thyme**
2 **bay leaves**
1 cup of **peeled carrots**, diced into ¼-inch pieces
2 medium **potatoes**, diced into ½-inch pieces
¾ cup of **coconut milk**
2 tablespoons of **lime juice**
Salt and **freshly ground black pepper**

In a saucepan large enough to hold the lamb in a single layer, heat the oil over medium heat. Dry the lamb with paper towels and gently season it with salt and black pepper. Lightly sauté it for about 5 minutes, until it's golden brown on all sides. As each batch is done, place it in a bowl.

When the lamb is browned, drain the fat from the saucepan and replace it with the butter. Melt the butter over moderate heat, then add the onion and celery, and cook, uncovered, stirring for about 5 minutes or until it's tender. Add the garlic, curry powder and cumin, and sauté for about 2 minutes, allowing the spices to cook.

Add the tomato paste, then whisk in the chicken broth, thyme, and bay leaf. Return the lamb to the saucepan, and add the carrots and potatoes. Bring the liquid to a boil over medium heat, then cover and simmer over low heat, with the lid ajar, for 1 hour or until the lamb and the vegetables are tender.

Allow it to rest for 5 minutes, and skim the excess fat from the surface. Strain the juice into another pot, and discard the bay leaf.

Over high heat, boil the juices down until 1 cup remains. Adjust the seasoning to taste. Add the coconut milk, and return the meat and vegetable solids to the pot, and simmer the stew to reheat.

Stir in the lime juice and season with salt and pepper to taste. (I know you just tested the seasoning, but I check it often during the cooking process.)

Serve over plain boiled rice or jasmine rice and garnish with cilantro and fried bananas.

Babootie

A South African tradition
Serve with chutney and rice.

Serves 6

2 pounds of **ground beef**
2 medium **sweet onions**
2 tablespoons of **butter**
1 cup of **cream** or **half and half**
3 **eggs**
2 slices of **white bread**, cubed
¼ cup of **dried apricots**, diced
1 **apple**, grated
¼ cup of **raisins**
¼ cup of **almonds**
2 tablespoons of **apricot jam**
1 tablespoon of **curry**
2 tablespoons of **lemon juice**
¼ teaspoon of **turmeric**
6 **bay leaves**
16 ounces of **canned tomatoes**

Sauté the beef in half of the butter until it's done, then remove it from the pan, leaving the juices. Add the onions and sauté them with curry powder until they are tender. Mix them with the meat.

In a bowl, mix half the cream, 1 egg, and the bread, mashing it with a fork. Add the apricots, raisins, almonds, jam, and lemon juice, and season with salt and pepper. Mix well. Add the meat mixture and mix well.

Prepare the topping by mixing 2 eggs, half the cream, and turmeric.

Grease an 8 x 12-inch ovenproof dish, and pour the mixture in, pressing the bay leaves into the top. Bake uncovered for 30 minutes in a 350-degree oven. Remove the dish from the oven, and add the topping.

Cook for 10 minutes, until the topping has set.

Lemon-Herb Marinated Roast Chicken

Alternatively, this marinade can be used on boneless chicken breasts and grilled.

Serves 2–4

1 3- to 4-pound **chicken** or 8 bone-in chicken breast halves
1 **Spanish onion**, cubed
1 cup of **fresh basil leaves**
½ cup of **fresh Italian parsley leaves**
2 tablespoons of **fresh rosemary leaves**
1 tablespoon of chopped **fresh sage**
2 tablespoons of **fresh mint leaves**
The grated zest of 1 **lemon**
2 teaspoons of **salt**
½ teaspoon of **pepper**
½ cup of **olive oil**

In a food processor, combine the onion, herb leaves, lemon peel, salt, and pepper. Pulse it until it's coarsely chopped. With the machine running, gradually add the olive oil, and process it until it's liquefied.

Pour this marinade over the chicken in a large bowl or heavy zip-top plastic bags, turning to coat all the chicken. Marinate 6–8 hours or overnight, turning occasionally.

Preheat the oven to 400.

Roast the whole chicken on a rack in a pan for 45–60 minutes (less if using halves) or until the juices run clear.

Garnish with fresh herbs.

Aruban Bread Pudding with Rum Sauce

Serves 4-6

5 slices of **white bread**, allowed to dry overnight
1 cup of **milk**
½ cup of **sugar**
¼ cup of **honey** (warmed)
3 **eggs**
1 tablespoon of **vanilla extract**
½ cup of **raisins**, soaked in rum for at least 30 minutes
½ cup of **dried cranberries**
1 tablespoon of **baking powder**

Remove the crust from the bread slices. Tear the bread into small pieces and put them in a bowl. Add milk and mash with a fork. Let the mixture stand for 1 hour.

Preheat the oven to 350. Lightly coat a loaf pan with butter.

Add sugar, honey, eggs, vanilla extract, fruits, and baking powder to the bread mixture. (As an option, add 2 ounces of roughly chopped white chocolate.) Mix well and pour into the loaf pan.

Place the pan in the oven and bake for 50–60 minutes, until the top is golden brown. Remove and let the pan cool on a wire rack.

Rum Sauce

1 tablespoon of **cornstarch**
½ cup of **sugar**
1¾ cups of **milk**
⅓ cup of **rum**
4 tablespoons of **unsalted butter**
½ teaspoon of **vanilla extract**

Mix the cornstarch and the sugar in a saucepan. Over medium heat, gradually add the milk and the rum, stirring constantly. Stir until the mixture almost starts to boil, then reduce the heat. Allow it to simmer, uncovered, for about 3 minutes, stirring occasionally. Add the butter and vanilla, and remove it from the heat.

Slice the bread pudding, and serve it with rum sauce.

Vintner Dinners

Over the years, we had the privilege of hosting a number of events that created special memories for everyone involved. Before I highlight a few of these, let me tell you my perspective about wine. I believe there are a lot of ridiculous assumptions connected with wine that confuse and scare people. For instance, some people insist on sniffing the cork, but there's no need to do that when they can smell the wine itself. Some people believe they have to follow the straightjacket rule to serve white wine with fish and chicken and red wine with meats, but that's only a rule of thumb. People should drink what they enjoy.

Years ago, I went on a hunting trip with a group of men to a ranch in Uvalde in South Texas. I cooked and brought the wine for dinner one night. The wine was Château Lafite Rothschild 1967 (Magnum). When I poured glasses for the men, one of them took his glass back into the kitchen. The rest of us heard ice clinking and the fizz of a soda bottle. When he walked back in, he announced, "Now it tastes better!" It didn't matter that no one else in the world would put 7UP in such a fine wine; it only mattered that he liked it better that way. (But the rest of us will never forget it!)

If these arcane rituals were jettisoned, the world of wine would be a lot more fun and far less intimidating. To unmask the world of wine, we hosted wine classes and special wine tastings.

Château Margaux

Of all the dinners we ever held, our Château Margaux dinner was the most renowned. When we hosted this dinner, the owner of the vineyard had recently died, and his 26-year-old daughter, Corinne Mentzelopoulos-Petit, was running it. We invited her, the winemaker, and their consultant, Professor Emile Peynaud, to join us, so they flew over for our dinner.

We had 34 vintages for our guests that night, and we flew one of them, a bottle from 1900, on Air France to Houston especially for the occasion. The dinner was invitation only, and we invited people from all across the country who appreciated Château Margaux. My favorite wine of the evening was the bottle of 1900. This shows that the less wine is moved around, the better its quality. My favorite moment of the evening occurred after we opened the middle flight, the wines of the 40's and 50's, when the aroma of these wines filled the room.

Wines of the 60's

Another evening, we hosted a dinner featuring the wines of the 60's. Two of the best French vintages of the entire 20th century were 1961 and 1966. To showcase the wines from this decade, we served a vintner dinner with 18 wines. It was a wonderful evening for the 35 people who came. One of my most vivid memories, beyond people enjoying the delicious food and wonderful wines, was the sheer number of glasses we used. I can still remember the sea of empty glasses that ended up back in the kitchen to be washed: over 600!

Taillevent in Houston

In 1994, a guest who often enjoyed our restaurant wanted us to host a fundraiser for The Children's Assessment Center in Houston. He's a world traveler, and he had dined at the Taillevent in Paris, one of the finest in the world. His idea was to bring the taste of Taillevent to Houston for the fundraising dinner.

He and I flew to Paris to have dinner at the restaurant. We met with the owner and the chef to talk about our plans, and they agreed to participate. A few months later, the owner and the chef flew to Houston for the event. We charged $500 per person, and those who attended enjoyed a dining experience of a lifetime.

The restaurant's attention to detail and commitment to excellence has left a lasting impression on my life.

Poodle Skirts and Flattops

At the restaurant, many of our guests had wonderful memories of growing up in the '50s, and they connected with the characters on "Happy Days." The era of President Eisenhower and the Edsel was a more relaxed time in our history before the massive cultural changes of the 60's. To capture this special time for our guests, we found the wines with the best vintages from that decade, such as Château Haut Brion 1953, Château Lafite Rothschild

1959, and Château Margaux 1955, and we set up the restaurant with a retro 50's theme: We put a motorcycle (à la Fonzie) in the middle of the room and arranged tables around it. We decorated with palm trees and played songs by the Beach Boys.

For months before the dinner, we gave fliers to guests to let them know about it. We encouraged those who made reservations to find (or make) clothes they had worn during the 50's (we wanted to advertise early to give them enough time to get their clothes ready). The menu that night included dishes which were revolutionary at the time and soon became favorites in fine restaurants everywhere: Steak Diane and Shrimp Scampi.

The motorcycle was the focal point. When people walked in, that was the first thing they saw, and when the Houston Chronicle wrote an article about the dinner, they were more enthusiastic about the motorcycle than anything else. That night, I learned two lessons: People love to connect with happy memories of their youth, and a single great prop can make an event.

I loved every aspect of creating these dinners for our guests. I enjoyed the initial concept, the promotion, preparation, presentation, and the delight of each guest. At the end of each of these dinners, we had many more empty bottles to remind us of our time together. Some people, I'm sure, would feel overwhelmed by all the details and the pressure to pull a fine dinner like this together, but for me, it fit my personality, talents, and desires. I always wanted to give people more than they possibly imagined. The look on their faces told me it was worth all the effort.

The French/American Wine Challenge

Charley's Wine Cellar
July 20, 1983
Dinner 8:00 p.m.

Gougère

Yields about 5 dozen 2-inch puffs.

½ teaspoon of **salt**
6 tablespoons of **unsalted butter**, cut into ¼-inch cubes
¾ cup of **water**
¾ cup, plus 2 tablespoons, of **all-purpose flour**
4 **large eggs**
4 ounces of grated **Gruyère cheese**

Fit a large pastry bag with a ½-inch round decorating tip. Lightly grease a large baking sheet and dust it lightly with flour. Put the rack in the lower third of the oven, and preheat to 400 for at least 20 minutes before baking.

Sift the flour and set it nearby. In a 1½-quart saucepan, bring the salt, butter, and water to a rolling boil over medium heat. Immediately remove it from the heat and stir to combine the ingredients in the pan. Add the flour all at once, stirring vigorously with a wooden spoon and scraping the sides of the pan until a stiff paste forms and comes together in a ball. Return the pan to medium heat, stirring quickly for about 10 seconds to eliminate any extra moisture. Remove the pan from the heat. The paste should be smooth, thick, and glossy. Transfer the thick paste to a large mixing bowl to cool for no more than 10 minutes.

Using an electric mixer, add all the eggs and the grated cheese to the dough, and beat at medium speed until the eggs and cheese are completely incorporated. (It should be smooth, glossy, and stiff, yet fall slowly in a ribbon effect when dropped from a spoon.)

Fill the pastry bag with the paste, and pipe bite-size cheesy puffs about 1 inch in diameter. Space the cheesy puffs ½-inch apart to allow for expansion. (Form them larger if you prefer. Alternatively, you can drop the paste from a spoon rather than pipe the mixture from a pastry bag.)

Dip a pastry brush into a small amount of water and glaze each puff lightly with water. The brush helps shape each one smoothly.

Bake about 20–25 minutes, until they are golden and the sides are rigid enough so they won't collapse when you remove them from the oven. Remove the baking sheet from the oven and place the sheet on a cooling rack.

THE MENU

Gougère

Spinach and Watercress Soup

Rack of Lamb

Baked Alaska

Spinach and Watercress Soup

A hit!

Serves 6

1 **leek,** chopped (white part only)
1 **onion,** chopped
2 tablespoons of **olive oil**
1 small **white potato,** peeled and sliced
1 cup of **frozen spinach**
2 bunches of **watercress**
3 cups of **chicken stock**
Salt and **ground black pepper** to taste
1 cup of **heavy whipping cream**

Gently sweat the chopped leek and the chopped onion in oil until they become soft, about 3 minutes—don't let them brown.

Add the potato slices and continue to cook 4–5 minutes. Add the spinach and cleaned watercress, and cook, stirring continuously until they are tender.

Add the stock and a pinch of salt and pepper. Bring it to a boil, and simmer gently for about 10 minutes.

Allow the soup to cool, and purée one-half of the soup at a time in a blender or food processor until it's very smooth. Don't strain it—that takes all the goodness away. Stir in the heavy cream. Adjust the seasoning and consistency (use a light chicken broth to thin if necessary).

Serve with a garnish of small shrimp fritters, inexpensive black caviar, or three-cheese tortellini.

Rack of Lamb

Serve with ratatouille and red wine sauce and potato pancakes.

Serves 2

1 full rack of **lamb,** trimmed
1 teaspoon of **salt**
1 teaspoon of **black pepper**
1 tablespoon of **Dijon mustard**
1 tablespoon of minced **garlic**
2 tablespoons of **fresh rosemary,** chopped
1 tablespoon of **olive oil**
½ cup of **breadcrumbs**

Mix salt, pepper, Dijon mustard, garlic, chopped rosemary, and olive oil. Spread the mixture over the rack of lamb and refrigerate for 2 hours.

Preheat the oven to 425. Allow the rack to come to room temperature for 30 minutes.

Heat a large, heavy, ovenproof skillet over medium-high heat. Place the rack of lamb in the skillet, turning it frequently for 2–3 minutes on all sides. (This step can be done in advance.)

Rub the topside of the rack of lamb with breadcrumbs until it's evenly coated. Cover the ends of the bones with foil to prevent burning.

Place the rack bone side down in a baking pan. Add extra breadcrumbs. Roast the lamb in the oven for 12 minutes per pound to get to medium. Remove it from the oven when the desired doneness is reached. Let it rest, loosely covered, for 5 minutes before carving between the ribs and serving.

Baked Alaska

Serves 4

4 circles of **Génoise or pound cake**, 3 inches by ½ inch
4 scoops of **ice cream** (try different flavors)
4 **egg whites**
A pinch of **salt**
¼ cup of **granulated sugar**
1 teaspoon of **cream of tartar**
½ teaspoon of **vanilla**
2 ounces of **raspberry liqueur or Kahlúa**

Make sure the ice cream is well frozen.

Preheat the oven to 450. Beat the egg whites until they foam. Add salt, cream of tartar, and vanilla, gradually beating in the sugar until shiny peaks form.

Moisten the cake circles with raspberry liqueur or Kahlúa. Place 1 scoop of ice cream on each circle. Cover each with a layer of meringue, using a spatula. Creatively decorate each one.

Bake 3 minutes at 450 until the edges of the meringue turn brown.

Backstage

When a theater or concert venue had a celebrity in for an evening or a week, they often asked us to cater a meal—but it wasn't as much fun as you might think. We cooked dinners for Tina Turner, Van Halen, Elton John, Jimmy Buffett, and many others. Each performer's contract included a rider describing the meals they required, with exact specifications about the foods they wanted. We didn't get to interact with many of these high-profile celebrities. In most cases, we talked only with their managers, who often were quite eccentric.

Actually, our first foray into the world of backstage catering was a disaster. We received an order for a dinner for 40 people. I was in New York at the time, and my assistant manager told me about it over the phone. We discussed cooking Chicken Italian, and I told her that she could expect to get eight pieces from each bird. I didn't go over the total amounts of each dish for her, and for some reason, she assumed that people would eat only one piece of chicken. She showed up to feed 40 people with five chickens. Jesus could have done it, but she couldn't. There were a lot of hungry people that night. It wasn't the happiest moment in our catering business. We recovered, however, and our catering business became successful.

Wild Mushroom Crepes

Makes 16 crepes

1½–2 pounds (total) of **fresh mushrooms,** sliced—you can mix Button, Shitake, Crimini, Oyster, or Cepes (but not Portobello)
2 tablespoons of **butter**
1 tablespoon of **garlic**, chopped
2 tablespoons of **cream sherry**
Freshly-grated **nutmeg**
Salt and **pepper** to taste
⅓ cup of **heavy cream**
½ cup of **sour cream**
8 ounces of **goat cheese**
16 **crepes**
Garnish with sour cream and grated **Monterey Jack cheese**

Preheat the oven to 350. Slice the mushrooms. In a large pan, sauté the mushrooms (one type at a time) in a small amount of butter over medium-high heat until the moisture evaporates.

Transfer the mushrooms to a large container. When all the mushrooms have been sautéed, add the garlic with a small amount of butter to the pan, and sauté for about one minute.

Drain the mushrooms, and add them back to the pan with the garlic. Add the sherry and the heavy cream, and season with nutmeg, salt, and pepper.

Gently heat the mixture until it's reasonably dry, and then remove it from the heat. The mixture can be refrigerated for several days.

When you're ready to prepare the crepes, thinly spread about a teaspoon of sour cream in a 1-inch strip about 2 inches from the crepe side. Crumble about a teaspoon of the chèvre (goat

cheese) on top of the sour cream. Add 1–2 tablespoons of the mushroom mix, and roll the crepe.

Lay the crepes in a buttered Pyrex dish side by side. Top the crepes with a thin layer of heavy cream, followed by finely shredded Monterey Jack cheese.

Bake at 400 until the cheese is melted, about 10–15 minutes.

Options to consider:

Salmon crepes: Mix canned salmon, mayonnaise, chopped pickles, and dill—the mixture should be firm.

Chicken crepes: Add finely minced chicken to the mushroom mixture or combine it with sour cream and chives.

Ground beef crepes: Brown 1 pound of ground beef with 3 tablespoons of chutney curry powder and grated onion. Put this filling in the crepes. Roll them and fry them in a mixture of half olive oil and half clarified butter. Sauté on both sides until they're crispy (but not too crispy).

Crepes

4 **eggs**
1 cup of **all-purpose flour**
½ cup of **milk**
½ cup of **water**
½ teaspoon of **salt**
2 tablespoons of **melted butter**

Put all the ingredients in a blender, and blend for 30 seconds. Scrape down the sides, and blend for 15 seconds more. Cover the blender jar, and let it sit for 1 hour. (This helps the flour absorb more of the liquids.)

Heat the crepe pan. Lightly grease the pan. Measure about ¼ cup of batter into the pan, and tilt the pan to spread the batter. Once the crepe has lots of little bubbles, loosen the edges with a spatula, and flip it over. The second side cooks quickly. Slide the crepe from the pan to a plate.

RECIPES

Wild Mushroom Crepes

Chicken Marengo

Studded Sirloin

Apple Strudel

Chicken Marengo

Serve with new potatoes in parsley butter and glazed baby carrots and petit pois.

Serves 10

½ cup of **all-purpose flour**
2 teaspoons of **salt**
Freshly ground pepper
½ teaspoon of dried **basil** or 2 teaspoons of fresh basil
½ teaspoons of dried **thyme** or 2 teaspoons of fresh thyme
½ teaspoon of dried **tarragon** or 2 teaspoons of fresh tarragon
½ teaspoon of **paprika**
10 boneless **chicken breasts**
¼ cup of **vegetable oil**
4 tablespoons of **butter**
A pinch of **sugar**
1 cup of **dry white wine**
2 tablespoons of **tomato paste**
1–1½ cups of **chicken stock**
1 large can of **Italian tomatoes**, either sliced or whole tomatoes halved and seeded (reserve a little of the liquid)
¾–1 pound of **fresh mushrooms**, halved or quartered
2 cloves of **garlic**, finely chopped
Parsley for sprinkling over the chicken

Combine the flour, seasoning, herbs, and paprika in a large plastic bag. Rinse, dry, and cut the chicken into approximately 1½-inch pieces. Drop the pieces into the bag of seasoned flour. Close and toss.

Add oil and butter to a large skillet over moderate heat. Sauté the chicken in batches until it's golden on all sides, and transfer it to a casserole dish.

Add any remaining flour to the fat in the skillet and stir it for 1 minute. Gradually add the wine, stir to deglaze drippings in the pan, and reduce by half over moderate heat. Stir in the tomato paste and stock, and simmer until it thickens. Add a little sugar to the sauce, and taste for seasoning.

Preheat the oven to 350. While it's heating, add tomatoes, mushrooms, and garlic, and mix these carefully into the sauce. Pour the sauce over the chicken, and mix it again. The liquid should barely cover the chicken. If necessary, add a little of the reserved tomato liquid.

Cover the casserole and bake it for 30–40 minutes, or until the chicken is tender. Sprinkle it with chopped parsley and serve it on individual plates, or spoon it into large volume au vent cases and sprinkle with parsley.

Studded Sirloin

Great with wasabi or au gratin mashed potatoes and grilled asparagus

Serves 6–8

2 1-pound **top sirloins**
4 tablespoons of **Clive's Rub or Montreal seasoning**
3 **garlic** cloves, sliced into slivers
1 tablespoon of **sea salt**

With a pairing knife, make 7 incisions in each steak and stud them with garlic slivers. Roll the steaks in a blend of the rub and a tablespoon of salt. Marinate for 30 minutes at room temperature before grilling.

Grill to required doneness. Let the steaks rest for 5 minutes, then add the sauce and serve.

Sauce

1 cup of **light red wine**
1 **shallot**
2 **sprigs of thyme**, pulled
6 **peppercorns**, whole
2 tablespoons of **butter**
2 ounces of **bittersweet chocolate**, shredded

Combine the wine, thyme, and peppercorns in a saucepan. Over medium heat, reduce the mixture until it's almost dry. Whisk in the butter. Don't let it boil, but keep it over a warm burner. Whisk in the chocolate.

Strain the mixture and swirl it on the plates with the steaks (just a little is needed).

Apple Strudel

Serve with vanilla bean ice cream and a dash of raspberry sauce.

Serves 8

1 pound of **sweet apples,** peeled, cored, and thinly sliced
¼ cup of **golden raisins**
¼ cup of **dried currants**
½ teaspoon of **ground cinnamon**
2 tablespoons of **light brown sugar**
½ cup **panko breadcrumbs**
½ package (16 ounces) of **phyllo dough**
¼ cup of **butter**, melted
Optional: add some **dried cranberries**

Preheat the oven to 400.

In a bowl, combine apples, raisins, currants, cinnamon, sugar, and bread crumbs. Stir it well.

Spread 2 sheets of pastry. Brush them with melted butter, and lay them on top of each other on a flat clean surface, Spread the fruit mixture evenly over the top sheet, then roll the sheets up to form a log.

Store the log in the refrigerator with slightly damp paper towels on top. Brush with melted butter again, and allow it to sit at room temperature for 10 minutes before baking.

Bake for 30 minutes, until the pastry is golden brown.

You can make strudel in advance and reheat it when you want to serve it.

2 for 2

Tea for two

In our culture, couples are waiting longer to start having children, and those of us who are a few years older have empty nests for a long time because we are living so much longer. In both cases, people find themselves cooking for two. For years, I've taught classes about how to cook delicious meals for two without being extravagant, but also without settling for sandwiches or microwave dinners.

Even more important, I've taught couples to cook together so they enjoy cooking and enhance their relationship. Cooking is a microcosm of life. In great restaurant kitchens, the chef and cooks know each other and their responsibilities so well that they don't even have to use words to communicate. When two people cook as a team, they have to communicate clearly, often, and graciously. After a while, each person instinctively knows what the other is going to do next. When preparing a meal, mistakes and accidents happen, and the couple needs to respond to one another with poise and grace.

Our life and health depends on the quality of our relationships. The goal of cooking isn't to just get a meal to eat, but to provide a shared experience so people talk and laugh, interacting about the monumental things as well as the small things in life. And the process of cooking together is more important than the end product of the dishes on the table. To cook together, be flexible, be patient, be creative, and above all, don't take yourself too seriously—laugh a lot.

Crabcakes

Serve one crabcake per person with garlic mayonnaise, herb butter, or mango salsa.

Serves 6

1 tablespoon of **clarified butter**
2 teaspoons of **onion,** diced
1 clove of **garlic,** chopped
1 tablespoon of **yellow bell
    pepper,** diced
1 tablespoon of **red bell pepper,**
    diced
½ small **serrano pepper,** minced
½ cup of **heavy cream**
1 teaspoon of **dry mustard**
1 teaspoon of **whole-grain
    mustard**
Juice and zest of half a **lemon**
2 teaspoons of **chives,** chopped
1 **egg yolk**
8 ounces of **crabmeat**
1¼ cup of **panko breadcrumbs**
Salt and **pepper**

Sauté the onion and gar-lic until they're tender (don't brown them). Add the peppers and cook for 2 minutes. Add cream, mustard, and lemon juice, and reduce by half. Season with salt, pepper, and chives.

Allow the mixture to cool, and then add it to the egg yolk.

Clean the crabmeat and fold it into the cream mixture.

Add enough breadcrumbs to bind the mixture (approximately 1 cup), and mold it into 2½-ounce cakes. Coat the cakes with the remaining breadcrumbs, and sauté them in clarified butter on both sides until they are golden brown.

Salmon on a Cedar Plank

Serves 4

1 **cedar plank**
4 6-ounce pieces of **salmon** (skin on)
1 tablespoon of **black pepper**
¼ teaspoon of **cayenne pepper**
½ teaspoon of **Aleppo chili**
½ teaspoon of **paprika**
½ teaspoon of **garlic powder**
½ teaspoon of **kosher salt**
⅛ cup **Lyle's Golden Syrup or honey**
⅛ cup **rice wine vinegar**

Soak the board in the sink for about 1 hour.

Mix all the spices together with the syrup and vinegar, and rub them into the fish. Let it stand for 20 minutes.

Place the salmon, skin side down, on the wet plank. Place the plank and the fish on a medium-hot grill, and cook it for approximately 15 minutes.

Keep the grill covered so the plank can smolder, which will bring out the flavor.

Remove the plank and the fish from the grill, and allow it to rest for 5 minutes.

Scrape the skin and bloodline away. Serve with sides of polenta and grilled asparagus or a simple oriental coleslaw.

THE MENU

Crabcakes

Salmon on a Cedar Plank

Chicken Schnitzel

Coeur à la Crème with Sauce

Chicken Schnitzel

Serves 4

2 medium **chicken breasts,** split
½ cup of **all-purpose flour**
2 **eggs,** beaten
2 cups of **matzo meal** mixed with 2 tablespoons of **mixed green herbs** (your choice)
Salt, to taste
Ground black pepper, to taste
1 cup of **vegetable oil** or **canola oil**
1 **lemon,** sliced or cut into wedges for garnish

Place a piece of chicken on a sheet of plastic wrap, cover it with a second sheet of wrap, and use a meat pounder or the flat bottom of a small, heavy skillet to flatten the meat. Set the cutlet aside, and repeat the process with the remaining pieces.

Using 3 shallow dishes, such as pie plates or shallow soup bowls, place the flour in one, the beaten eggs in a second, and the matzo meal in the third. Season both sides of each cutlet liberally with salt and pepper, and working one cutlet at a time, dredge both sides in the flour, shake off excess, then dip both sides into the eggs (hold the cutlet above the dish for a moment to allow the excess egg to drip off), then dredge both sides in matzo meal, pressing them onto the surface to form an even coat.

Heat the oil in a heavy-bottom skillet or cast-iron pan. When the oil is hot, add cutlets one at a time. Cook them 2 minutes on each side or until they're golden brown.

Place the cooked cutlets on a non-stick oven pan. They may be refrigerated. When you want to serve them, bring them to room temperature and cook them in a 300-degree oven for 5 minutes.

Serve the cutlets with slice of lemon, and garnish with chopped fresh herbs.

Coeur à la Crème with Sauce

Serve with crème fraiche.

Serves 6

5 ounces of **cream cheese,** at room temperature
1 5-inch **vanilla bean** or ½ teaspoon of **pure vanilla extract**
¼ cup of **confectioner's sugar**
1 cup of **heavy cream**
1 pint of **strawberries**
¼ cup of **sherry**
¾ cup of **currant jelly**

Soften the cream cheese, and beat it with an electric beater.

Split the vanilla bean, and scrape the seeds into the cheese. Continue beating, gradually adding the sugar.

Whip the cream until it becomes stiff, and fold it into the cheese.

Rinse out six pieces of cheesecloth in cold water, and use them to line six small Coeur à la Crème molds. (Or you can use one large piece of cheesecloth to line a large mold.) Spoon equal portions of the cream mixture into the molds. Bring up the overlapping ends of the cheesecloth, and fold them lightly over the top of each portion of cheese. Chill thoroughly.

Meanwhile, trim, rinse, and drain the strawberries.

Blend the wine and jelly, and cook the mixture over low heat, stirring until it's blended and smooth. Combine this mixture with the strawberries.

Unmold the cheese onto chilled dessert plates. Serve the strawberries and crème fraiche on the side. Pass a sugar bowl for those who want it to be even sweeter.

Crème Fraiche

Makes about 1 cup

1 cup of **heavy cream**
1 tablespoon of **buttermilk**

Combine the cream and buttermilk in a jar with a screw top. Secure the top and shake the mixture for a second or two. Let it stand 8 to 12 hours, or until the cream is lightly thickened.

"Hallmark" Dinners

Anniversaries, birthdays, and Valentine's Day. You can create a wonderful, intimate dinner for the special occasions when many people give each other Hallmark cards . . . and you won't need your local five-star restaurant. The two nights I'd recommend that couples never go out to eat are New Year's Eve and Valentine's Day. At our restaurant, we were so crowded on these nights that we had difficulty giving people food and service up to our standards. Instead, go out to dinner the night before, the night after, or to stay at home and cook something special for the one you love.

For intimate dinners, think about what pleases him or her. Make a list of those things: type and color of flowers, style of silverware, dishes, tablecloth, appetizer, salad, main dish, dessert, candles, music, lighting . . . everything. Then create a special evening. If she loves stone crab, find the best and freshest ones you can buy. I did some research to find the best source of stone crab. I called a man in Florida, and he took my call from the dock where his boat had just tied up. He was coming in with the nicest, freshest stone crabs I could buy, so I had him ship me some that day. If she likes Casablanca lilies, buy a bunch of those along with a few roses to add color and texture.

Don't just buy prepared foods and prearranged flowers. We demonstrate the depth

of our love when we take the time to prepare the food ourselves, and we show we care when we buy bunches of several kinds of flowers and a vase so we can arrange the bouquet ourselves. If the food isn't as good as it would be if a chef cooked it, it doesn't matter. And if the flower arrangement is a bit out of balance, don't worry about it. The fact that you cooked and arranged the flowers yourself demonstrates the reality of your love, and that's what counts.

Spinach Salad with Goat Cheese

Serves 4

Dressing

4 ounces of **light olive oil**
3 cloves of **garlic,** quartered
1 **bay leaf**
1 tablespoon of **fresh thyme**
2 sprigs of **rosemary**
5 **whole black peppercorns**
1 3-ounce log of **goat cheese**
1 medium **shallot,** peeled and sliced
2 ounces of **balsamic vinegar**
1 teaspoon of **light brown sugar**
Salt and **pepper**

Salad

4 cups of **fresh baby spinach**
½ cup of **walnuts,** toasted in **vegetable oil** and **sea salt**
1 tablespoon of **vegetable oil**

Preheat the oven to 400. In a glass or ceramic dish, combine all the ingredients of the dressing—leave the cheese whole. Cover with foil and bake for about 30 minutes, or until the shallots are tender.

Allow the mixture to cool for 15 minutes, and then remove the cheese. Pour the contents of the baking dish through a strainer over a small saucepan. Remove the shallot, chop it, and add it into dressing.

Season the dressing with salt and pepper.

In a small bowl, mix walnuts with vegetable oil and sea salt. Toast the walnuts on a baking sheet at 375 until they are fragrant, about 5 minutes.

To serve, mix the spinach with warmed dressing. Sprinkle the goat cheese on the spinach, and scatter the toasted walnuts on top. You can also mix the cheese with the dressing before mixing with spinach to enhance the flavor of the goat cheese.

THE MENU

Spinach Salad with
Goat Cheese

Snapper with
Crab Provencale

Sautéed Spaghetti Squash

Bananas Foster

Snapper with Crab Provençale

Serve with steamed spaghetti squash and oven-roasted new potatoes.

Serves 4

4 **snapper fillets,** 6–7 ounces each (yellow tail snapper is best, but red snapper is very good, too)
Seasoned flour (see below)
¼ cup of clarified **butter**

Seasoned flour

1 cup of **all-purpose flour**
1 teaspoon of **paprika**
1 teaspoon of **sea salt**
1 teaspoon of **white pepper**
½ teaspoon of **curry powder**

Clean and wash the snapper fillets, and dip each piece in seasoned flour. Melt the clarified butter in a thick-bottomed skillet. Sauté each fillet for 1–2 minutes over medium heat, then turn and repeat. To ensure that the fish cooks evenly, the heat shouldn't be too high. Remove the fillets from the pan and place them on a non-stick or buttered baking pan. (You may want to complete this step in advance and keep the cooked fillets in the refrigerator until you're ready to complete the dish.)

Heat the oven to 400, and cook the snapper for 3–5 minutes (depending on the thickness of the fillets). Don't overcook them! Check for doneness with a pairing knife.

Place the fish on a plate and spoon Crab Provençale over the top and sides.

Beurre Blanc

½ cup of **white wine**
1 small **bay leaf**
1 tablespoon of **white vinegar**
6 whole **black peppercorns**
¼ cup of **heavy cream**
¼ pound of **unsalted butter,** cut into pieces

Reduce the wine, vinegar, bay leaf, and black peppercorn mixture until the liquid is almost gone, and then add the cream. Reduce this by half, then whisk in the butter in small pieces. Strain and season.

Don't boil the liquid at any time, and don't allow it to get cold. Keep the pan on a very low burner until you need it to complete the Crab Provençale. Beurre Blanc can be made an hour in advance.

Crab Provençale

1 small **shallot,** chopped
2 ounces of **dry white wine**
2 tablespoons of chopped and seeded **tomatoes**
4–6 ounces of cleaned **lump crabmeat**
1 teaspoon of chopped **chives**

Cook the shallot in white wine and reduce it until it's almost dry. Add tomatoes and continue to cook for 2–3 minutes, and then sprinkle in the chives.

Add Beurre Blanc to the mixture, and then fold in the lump crabmeat—add it gently to preserve the lumps of meat.

Test for seasoning.

Sautéed Spaghetti Squash

1 medium **spaghetti squash**
4 ounces of **butter**
1 tablespoon of **salt**
1 tablespoon of **chicken bouillon powder or cube**
Salt and **pepper** to taste

Slice the squash lengthwise, and remove the seed mass with a tablespoon. In a 4-quart pot, heat 2 quarts of water with a tablespoon of salt and 1 tablespoon of chicken bouillon (with no MSG). Gently place both halves of the squash skin side down in the boiling water, and cover tightly. Cook 20–30 minutes, until the squash is tender.

Remove the squash from the pot and allow it to cool to room temperature. Use a fork to scrape the squash from the skin in strings.

Melt the butter in a skillet and add the strings of spaghetti squash. (It's best to cook this dish in half batches, so use half the butter and half the squash at a time.) Stir continually until it's hot, and then season to taste. Serve immediately.

If you want to cut down on carbohydrates, spaghetti squash can be a substitute for spaghetti or any other pasta.

Bananas Foster

Serves 2

2 tablespoons of **butter**
⅓ cup of **brown sugar**
2 ounces of **rum**
2 **bananas,** cut 1-inch pieces
1 teaspoon of **cinnamon**
1 ounce of **orange juice**
2 scoops of **vanilla ice cream**
Optional: garnish with **toasted almonds**

Combine the butter and brown sugar in a thick-bottomed sauté pan. Cook over medium heat, stirring frequently until the sugar dissolves.

Place the bananas in the pan, turning often. When bananas begin to brown, move the pan away from the stovetop and carefully add the rum. Bring the pan back to the stovetop. If you're using gas, the liquid should light when the pan is slightly tilted toward the flame. Sprinkle with cinnamon.

Add the orange juice and continue to cook the sauce until it thickens slightly, 1–2 minutes. Remove the bananas from the pan and serve them over portions of ice cream.

Generously spoon warm sauce over the top of ice cream and serve immediately.

Fish off the Docks

People often ask me what's my favorite dish to cook — it's fresh fish. When I go fishing, I sometimes catch more than I can eat, so on the way home, I call some friends to come over and get some fish that evening. Years ago at the restaurant, we served some men who fished often and caught a lot of fish. When they found out how much I love fresh fish, they offered me some. On Sunday afternoons after a successful trip, they called me from the docks and told me what kinds and how much fish they wanted to bring me. Sometimes they had 400 pounds of fish, mostly snapper, mahi mahi, and amberjack. I knew it had been caught in the last day, so I bought them sight unseen. While they were on their way into town, I sent an email to our regular guests to let them know fresh fish would be on the menu Monday night. There's nothing better than fish that swam yesterday and is on your plate today.

At the restaurant, we grilled over pecan wood, but we also baked and pan-seared certain fish. White fish, like flounder or sea bass, is delicate and doesn't stand up to grilling. For these, baking or pan-searing is a much better way to cook them. And for these fish, the sauces and side dishes should be light, such as lime butter and a salad. Fish that have significant oil content, such as amberjack, or are dense, like tuna, can be grilled very easily. These fish go well with richer sauces and side dishes.

Match your cooking method to the fish's texture, and select accompanying dishes wisely. Fresh fish is a delight if it's prepared well and a disaster if it's not.

There's no point in serving fish unless it is absolutely fresh. Fresh fish is firm and its smell is clean. The fish's eyes should not be sunken and should be bright (not cloudy or bloody), and the gills should be bright red. If the fish is fresh, the body will be turned in a semi circle and the head turned towards the tail.

The most popular methods of cooking fish include:

Poaching uses a cooking liquid such as wine, court bouillon, or fish stock. This is the easiest method and produces the best results. Lightly season your fish fillet and place it in a buttered fish kettle or cast-iron pot. Cover the fish with white wine or fish stock. Bring it to a boil on top of the stove, then reduce the heat to medium, and cook until it is done (firm with a translucent color). Drain the liquid and reduce by half, and finish with fresh herbs of choice and a little butter or heavy cream.

Braising is usually used for whole or large pieces of fish. It involves cooking slowly in a small amount of liquid on a bed of root vegetables and spices. Butter the bottom and sides of a cast-iron or ovenproof dish large enough to hold the fish. Add a selection of finely chopped onions, garlic, carrots, celery, sliced mushrooms, and fresh herbs. Season the fish lightly on both sides with sea salt and white pepper. Place it on top of the vegetables, and spread some butter over the top. Add 1 part of white or red wine and 1 part of fish stock. Lightly cover with a piece of parchment (to allow some of the liquid to evaporate), and cook in a 400-degree oven, basting often. When the fish is done, it will be opaque and relatively firm but not hard to the touch. At that point, drain the liquid, and place the fish on a covered plate or platter. Reduce the liquid by half on top of the stove, then pour it over the fish and finish with a touch of butter or cream—you choose how much.

Pan-roasting is usually used for individual portions of small and flat fish (6–7 ounces each). Make sure the fish is clean and all the small bones are removed. Rub the fish with a few drops of light olive oil, and then roll it in seasoned flour, shaking off the excess. In a heavy-bottom skillet, heat 1 tablespoon of clarified butter for every 2 pieces of fish. Place the fish skin side up. Cook on medium-high heat for 3 minutes, rotate it about 45 degrees with a metal spatula, and continue cooking 3–4 more minutes. Turn the fish over, cooking the other side the same way. If the pan dries, add a little extra butter. Season each side with sea salt, and allow the fish to rest 3 minutes before serving.

Grilling is very popular, but the selection of fish is most important. Firm fish, such as tuna, salmon, or shark, can be cooked directly on the grill if it is handled carefully. The grill should be at medium-low to avoid overcooking. Most grilled fish benefits from wet marinades. If using a marinade, allow the fish to soak up flavor for at least 30 minutes, and refrigerate while the fish is soaking. If you want to grill delicate, white fish, use a dry rub or simple seasoning salt.

Remove excess marinade and place the fish skin-side down on the grill.

If you want to grill fish with its skin on, place it skin-side down on grill, and turn the fish only once. A 6–7 ounce pieces of fish should take 3–4 minutes on grill before turning, and then finish cooking for 3 minutes.

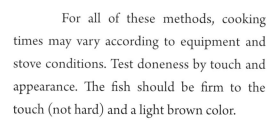

For all of these methods, cooking times may vary according to equipment and stove conditions. Test doneness by touch and appearance. The fish should be firm to the touch (not hard) and a light brown color.

Let me give you several recipes to serve with fish.

Avocado Relish

Makes 2 cups

1 tablespoon of **light olive oil**
1 small **red onion,** chopped
3 tablespoon of **rice wine vinegar**
1 teaspoon of **honey**
1 **poblano chili,** peeled, seeded, and finely chopped
2 medium **ripe avocadoes**
Salt and **pepper** to taste

To prepare the poblano pepper, dip it in olive oil and grill it on low heat, turning often. When it turns black, remove it from the heat and run it under cold water to loosen the skin.

Heat the oil in a small skillet over medium heat. Add the onion and sauté until it's softened, about 2 minutes. Stir in the vinegar, honey, and chilies, and remove the pan from heat to let it cool.

Before serving the relish, cut the avocado into small pieces. Place the avocado in a single layer in a shallow dish, and pour the onion mixture on top. Stir gently—don't mush the avocado. Season to taste with the salt and pepper.

RECIPES

Avocado Relish

Roasted Red Pepper Aioli

Thai Curry Vinaigrette

Mango Dressing

Sweet Pepper Dressing

Wasabi Aioli

Tomato-Caper Berry Relish

Papaya Relish

Roasted Red Pepper Aioli

1 **red bell pepper**
3 cloves of **garlic,** chopped
1 small **shallot,** chopped
1 ounce of **sherry (or white wine)**
1 ounce of **chicken broth**
6 ounces of **mayonnaise**
Salt and **pepper** to taste

Roast, seed, peel, and chop the red bell pepper, and put it in a large saucepan.

Combine the garlic, onions, shallots (all finely chopped), white wine, and chicken stock. Reduce the mixture until all the liquid is gone.

Blend in a blender or food processor until the purée is smooth. Cool, then add mayonnaise and mix well. Put it aside for 30 minutes to accentuate the flavors.

Thai Curry Vinaigrette

Great with salads or sprinkled over grilled fish or beef

½ cup of **olive oil**
¼ cup of **sesame oil**
1 teaspoon of **shallot,** finely chopped
1 teaspoon of **garlic,** chopped
¼ cup of **rice vinegar**
1 teaspoon of **red Thai paste**
1 teaspoon of grated **fresh ginger** mixed with ½ teaspoon (or more) of **curry powder**
½ teaspoon of **Dijon mustard**
Salt and **pepper** to taste

Heat the olive oil and sesame oil over low heat. Add the shallot and garlic, and sweat them (no color) for 2–3 minutes until they soften. Remove them from the stove and allow them to cool.

In a bowl, mix the vinegar, Thai paste, ginger, and Dijon mustard. Drizzle the oil into the vinegar mixture, and adjust the seasoning to taste.

Mango Dressing

Serve as a salad dressing or a sauce on grilled or fried fish.

1 cup of **fresh mango,** chopped
½ cup of **rice wine vinegar**
½ cup of **sugar**
¼ cup of **Thai chili sauce**
2 cups of **olive oil**

Blend all the ingredients in a blender or food processor until the dressing is smooth.

Wasabi Aioli

Serve with grilled fish.

1 tablespoon of **wasabi**
½ cup of **mayonnaise**
½ teaspoon of **garlic,** finely minced
The juice of 1 **lemon**
Salt and **white pepper**

Mix all the ingredients and keep it cold. Season with salt and white pepper to taste.

Tomato-Caper Berry Relish

4 vine-ripened **tomatoes,** seeded and diced
1 small **sweet onion** (1015 or Maui), finely chopped
½ cup of **flat leaf Italian parsley**
1 teaspoon of **sea salt**
2 ounces of **kalamata olives,** pitted and diced
2 ounces of **caper berries,** stem off and sliced
The juice of 1 **lemon**
4 ounces of **light olive oil**
Salt and **pepper** to taste

Mix the oil, lemon juice, and salt together. Add the rest of the ingredients and mix well. Allow it to marinate for 4 hours.

Serve at room temperature.

Sweet Pepper Dressing

Great with grilled tuna and slices of avocado or English cucumbers

3 **bell peppers** (1 each of orange, yellow, and red)
1 small **red onion**
1 **English hothouse cucumber**
½ cup of **light olive oil**
2 ounces of **balsamic vinegar**
Salt and **cracked black pepper** to taste
½ cup of your choice **fresh mixed herbs** (oregano, tarragon, basil, chives, and green
    onions), finely chopped

Cut all the peppers, onion, and cucumber into small pieces and place them in a bowl. In a separate bowl, mix the oil and vinegar, and season it with salt and cracked black pepper.

When you're ready to serve, mix the herbs, vegetables, and dressing.

Papaya Relish

1 **papaya,** cut in 1-inch pieces
⅓ **pineapple,** cut in ½ inch pieces
½ **red sweet pepper,** finely chopped
¼ **red onion,** finely chopped
¼ cup of **cilantro,** chopped (use more if you love it)
The juice of ½ **lemon**
The juice of 1 **lime**
Season with **salt, white pepper,** and **light brown sugar**
For extra flavor, add ¼ teaspoon of **cayenne pepper**

Mix all the ingredients, and season to taste.

The Two Unique Features of a Wedding

I've had the great privilege of marrying many couples. One of the questions I ask them in our conversations to prepare for the wedding is, "What are the most important aspects of the wedding to you?" In many cases, they talk about the ceremony being meaningful, creating a delightful time with friends and family, flowers, and the photographer. I agree. Beyond those aspects, I tell them that a wedding has two features that aren't found at any other event. They'll find similar foods, drink, dancing, gifts, friends, or many other things at other festivities, but they won't find a wedding dress and a wedding cake anywhere else. I advise them to make these unique features their priorities in their planning.

The beautiful bride is the focal point of the wedding. All eyes are on her from beginning to end, and her dress shows her beauty on her special day. The cake is the only unique food at a wedding, and it should receive the attention it is due. I recommend that couples spend more time, attention, and money making those features memorable.

Let me give you an idea to consider. Some people may think I'm eccentric, but I believe that much of the money spent on weddings today could be spent in better ways. The average cost of a wedding in America today is about $25,000. When I talk to young couples in love, I suggest they talk to the bride's parents about a new direction: They can have a very nice wedding for $3000 to $5000, and put the rest in savings to use as a down payment for a home, to start a new business, or to pay off college debts.

I've met with brides' parents to discuss ways to have a beautiful wedding and save money. On a few occasions, I've helped prepare the meal for the wedding in addition to conducting the ceremony. One time, the bride's father cooked for 150 guests and hosted them at home. To play during the dinner, he hired two students from a local university who were studying concert piano, and the music was phenomenal. On a few occasions, the bride's parents asked their friends to cook their favorite dishes for the reception. The parents were then free to focus on their out-of-town family members the day before and the morning of the wedding. The friends who cooked their specialties enjoyed being part of the special moment in the young couple's lives—and the food was fantastic!

Don't be stuck in a tradition that costs tens of thousands of dollars and is over in a few hours. Think about the couple's long-term future, not just the joy of the day. Spend money on the two unique things in a wedding ceremony, and launch the newly married couple on a lifetime of wisdom and love.

Sakowitz Shrimp Salad

2 pounds of medium (26 count) **shrimp,** peeled and boiled in **Creole seasoning mix**

1 **shallot,** finely chopped

2 cloves of **garlic,** minced

2 stalks **celery,** finely chopped

1 tablespoon of **fresh lemon juice**

2 cups of **mayonnaise**

1 tablespoon of **Worcestershire sauce**

1 tablespoon of **Creole mustard**

½ ounce of **anchovy paste**

A dash of **red pepper sauce (Tabasco)**

½ cup of cooked **spinach,** drained and finely chopped

2 **eggs,** boiled medium hard

Salt and **white pepper** to taste

Lightly mix the shrimp, celery, garlic, shallots, and lemon juice. Add salt and white pepper to taste.

Gently stir in the mayonnaise, Worcestershire sauce, mustard, anchovy paste, and pepper sauce. Add the spinach and eggs, and mix lightly.

Serve in lettuce cups or in avocados cut in half with the centers filled and overflowing.

Mushroom Bacon Quiche

Great for brunch

Serves 6–8

1 9-inch **deep-dish pie crust**
3 tablespoons of **butter**
1 tablespoon of **green onions,** chopped
4 ounces of **mushrooms,** washed and sliced
4 ounces of **cooked bacon,** roughly chopped
1 heaping cup of **Swiss cheese,** grated
6 **eggs,** beaten
1 pint of **half and half**

Preheat the oven to 375.

In a small skillet over medium heat, melt 2 tablespoons of butter, and sauté the onions and mushrooms until they're cooked (about 6 minutes).

Place even amounts of bacon, cheese, and vegetables in the bottom of the pie crust.

Melt the remaining butter in a skillet. In a large bowl, mix the beaten eggs and half and half. Fold in the remaining melted butter, and immediately pour the mixture into the pie crust. Bake at 375 for 30–40 minutes, or until a knife placed in center comes out clean.

Ribeye Roast

Serves 8-10

A 4–5 pound **ribeye roast**
3 tablespoons of **fresh garlic**
1 cup of **mushroom soy sauce**
4 ounces of **hoisin sauce**
½ cup of **grape jelly**
1 **baking bag**
Fresh or bottled **horseradish**

Place the roast in baking bag with the other ingredients except the horseradish and marinate overnight in the refrigerator. Remove it when you're ready to cook.

Preheat the oven to 375.

Allow approximately 90 minutes cooking time (20 minutes per pound) for a rare center.

After baking, drain the drippings into a large bowl, and allow it to cool in the refrigerator. Skim off the layer of fat. (The sauce can be saved in a glass jar. It makes a great marinade for beef, burgers or chicken.)

Serve the roast with horseradish.

A delicious side dish is a spinach salad dressed with mandarin oranges, walnuts, mushrooms, dried cranberries, and your favorite dressing, such as T. Marzetti's Original Spinach Salad Dressing. Good choices for vegetables are steamed asparagus or artichokes with a small amount of butter or olive oil.

Eggs Benedict ...with a Twist

Serves 4

1 medium **sweet potato**
¼ cup of **olive oil**
8 **eggs**
1 teaspoon of **distilled white vinegar**
4 ¼-inch thick pieces of **pastrami turkey,** grilled or heated in a skillet
½ teaspoon of **curry powder,** lightly toasted
½ teaspoon of **salt**

Preheat the oven to 375.

Wash the potato (but don't peel it), and cut it into 8 round pieces about ½-inch thick. Brush the potato pieces with olive oil, and sprinkle them with curry powder and salt. Place them on a non-stick oven pan, and cook them until they're tender (about 20 minutes).

While the potato is cooking, poach the eggs. To poach them, fill a large, thick-bottom saucepan with 3 inches of water. Bring the water to a gentle simmer, and then add the vinegar. Carefully break each of the eggs into a small glass container, and then gently place them individually in the simmering water. Allow them to cook for approximately 3 minutes. The yolks should still be soft in the center. Remove the eggs from the water with a slotted spoon, and put them on a warm plate.

Cut each piece of turkey in half. Lightly brown the turkey in a medium skillet or on the grill.

Place 2 pieces of potato on each plate, and top each one with a strip of turkey. Place an egg on top of the turkey, and then spoon Hollandaise Sauce on each egg. Very lightly dust each one with toasted curry powder, and serve immediately. (To toast curry powder, sprinkle it in a baking pan, and bake at 350 for 3 minutes.)

[see next page for Hollandaise Sauce recipe]

Hollandaise Sauce

4 **egg yolks**
3½ tablespoons of **lemon juice**
1 pinch of **ground white pepper**
⅛ teaspoon of **Worcestershire sauce**
1 tablespoon of **water**
1 cup of **butter,** melted

Fill the bottom of a double boiler part way with water. Make sure the water doesn't touch the top of the pan. Bring the water to a gentle simmer. In the top of the double boiler, whisk together the egg yolks, lemon juice, white pepper, Worcestershire sauce, and water.

Add the melted butter to the egg yolk mixture 1 or 2 tablespoons at a time while constantly whisking the yolks. If the sauce gets too thick, add a teaspoon or two of hot water. Continue whisking until all the butter is incorporated. Whisk in the salt, and then remove it from the heat. Place a lid on the pan to keep the sauce warm.

(Actually, I prefer to use hollandaise from a package, replace the water with milk, and finish with lemon juice to taste. It holds together at a higher temperature and reduces the oops factor.)

Brunch.org gives us a bit of history about the origins of Eggs Benedict. Actually, this site explains that there are two different stories about it, both dating from New York in the 1890s. The site says:

"One story names Delmonico's as the point of origin, in 1893. A Mrs. LeGrand Benedict (and possibly her husband) were tired of the usual fare at the restaurant, and negotiated the new dish with the help of the maître d'hôtel.

The more interesting story credits Mr. Lemuel Benedict, who requested toast, bacon, poached eggs, and a small pitcher of hollandaise to help treat a hangover one morning in 1894 at the Waldorf-Astoria. If true, Mr. Benedict also appears to have been the first to recognize the therapeutic effects of eggs Benedict.

So, take your pick: 1893 or 1894, downtown or midtown, restaurant or hotel, wife of the elite or Wall Street broker, fighting tedium or fighting intoxication."
—from www.brunch.org

Chicken Piccata

8 7- or 8-ounce **chicken breasts,** pounded thin
¼ cup of clarified **butter**
3 **garlic cloves,** roughly chopped
Seasoned flour
Salt and **freshly ground black pepper** to taste

Sauce

1 cup of **white wine**
¼ cup of **chicken stock**
1 **shallot,** chopped
1 teaspoon of **garlic,** chopped
3 **parsley** stalks
4 basil **leaves**
The zest of 1 **lemon**
½ pound of **sweet butter**
1 tablespoon of **parsley,** chopped
1 tablespoon of **capers**
1 teaspoon of **lemon juice**

Season the chicken breasts with salt, pepper, and olive oil, and allow them to sit at room temperature for 30 minutes.

Pass the chicken lightly through seasoned flour, and sauté them on each side in clarified butter with garlic (whole cloves) until they're golden brown.

For the sauce, reduce the wine, chicken stock, and herbs (shallot, garlic, basil, parsley stalks, and lemon zest) until it's ¼ cup. Remove the liquid from the stove, and whisk in the butter 1 tablespoon at a time. Reheat it if necessary, but don't let it boil. When all the butter has been added, strain it, and add chopped parsley, capers, and lemon juice to taste. Adjust the seasoning. Keep it warm in a bain-marie.

Serve with baby red potatoes roasted in rosemary and olive oil, and garlic sautéed spinach or grilled vegetables.

Strandelicious

Galveston, an island off the coast of Texas south of Houston, has a culture all its own. For a century, it was a thriving coastal port until the Great Storm of 1900 ravaged the city. In the years required to rebuild, many of the shipping companies decided to move into safer waters along the Houston Ship Channel, and Galveston's economy suffered. In recent years, though, Galveston has been regaining its charm.

It hosts the largest Mardi Gras celebration outside of New Orleans, as well as Dickens on the Strand each Christmas.

George Mitchell is one of the most influential land developers in Southeast Texas. I met Mr. Mitchell when I was catering and managing the restaurant, and he asked me to help manage six restaurants he owned in Galveston, from an upscale Charley's 517 at the Wentletrap to The Strand Brewery & Grill. Each restaurant has its own style and ambiance, and we needed to find a way to let people know about the uniqueness of each one. To feature all of our restaurants on or near The Strand (the main street in downtown Galveston), we promoted the flavor of them all with the word *Strandelicious*.

Cajun Barbequed Shrimp

Cajun, but not hot . . . and yes, you really do use that much butter!

Serves 8 as an appetizer

3 slices of **bacon,** cut into small strips
4 ounces of **unsalted butter**
2 tablespoons of **Dijon mustard**
1 teaspoon of **chili powder**
¼ teaspoon of **dried basil**
¼ teaspoon of **dried thyme**
Black pepper
Sea salt
1 tablespoon of **crab boil** (such as Zatarain's)
½ teaspoon of **red pepper sauce (Tabasco)**
1½ pounds of medium **shrimp** (26 count), shell on

Preheat the oven to 375.

Cook the bacon in a large ovenproof pot until it's brown. Add butter and let it melt. Add the remaining ingredients and place the pot, uncovered, in the oven. Bake for 20 minutes.

These shrimp are delicious served with toasted French bread.

Scrumptious Fried Shrimp

Serves 6

Peanut oil for frying
2 large **eggs**
½ cup of **buttermilk**
1 teaspoon of **salt**
2 pounds of fresh, small **shrimp,** peeled and deveined, with the tail intact
1 cup of **corn flour** or **matzo meal**

Pour 3 inches of oil into a stockpot or Dutch oven, and heat it over medium-high heat. Beat the eggs with the milk and salt. Dip the shrimp in the egg mixture, making sure they are evenly coated. Drain the shrimp in a sieve, and shake them well to remove excess.

Put the meal in a bowl. When the oil reaches 365, roll the shrimp in the meal, and shake off the excess. Fry the shrimp in small batches in the hot oil until they're golden brown (1–2 minutes). Remove the shrimp from the oil with a wire mesh strainer, and shake off all the excess oil.

Serve them immediately with remoulade and cocktail sauce.

Cocktail Sauce

The most important instruction for boiled shrimp is to use a good shrimp boil mix—and don't overcook them! The second most important instruction is to make an excellent cocktail sauce.

2–3 tablespoons of **raw horseradish,** finely grated
2 teaspoons of **dark brown sugar**
1 teaspoon of **fresh lemon juice**
1 cup of **ketchup**

Mix all the ingredients together, and add extra horseradish or brown sugar to taste.

Shrimp Scampi

Serves 4 as a main course

1 pound of medium (21 count) **shrimp**
4 ounces of **butter**
1 ounce of **olive oil**
4 large cloves of **garlic,** roughly chopped
3 ounces of **dry vermouth** or **white wine**
1 tablespoon of **chopped fresh parsley**
1 tablespoon of **chopped fresh chives**
 The juice of ½ **lemon**
Salt and **pepper** to taste

Peel, devein, and rinse the shrimp in cold water. Dry them on paper towels.

Heat the butter and oil over medium-high heat. Add the shrimp a few at a time and sauté them until they turn pink—don't overcook them!

Add garlic to the pan of shrimp and mix well, and then add the vermouth. Raise the heat to medium-high, and cook for 2–3 minutes, stirring or shaking the pan constantly.

Season with salt and pepper and chopped parsley (fresh basil works well, too). If the sauce is too thin, whisk in an ounce of butter.

Squeeze in the lemon juice, and serve immediately over rice pilaf or linguine.

Sabbath: Connecting Once Each Week

In the Jewish community, Sabbath contains many layers of meaning. God instituted the Sabbath for us as a day of rest and reflection—following his example of resting on the seventh day of creation. We're busy the other six days, but one day a week is set aside to think, read, rest, relax, and pray so that our lives line up with God's purposes for us. But Sabbath is also a time for families to connect with each other. If family

members passed each other with lightning speed during the rest of the week, they can now pause, come together, and enjoy each other. In my family when I was growing up, Sabbath was a time for us to talk, eat, and laugh together. Today, I have extended family in Israel, and on every Sabbath, they gather at one of their homes for dinner, backgammon, and lively discussions about whatever is on their minds. I've been there with them. It's a wonderful time for them to reconnect with those they love over a good meal and great conversation. I believe the Sabbath tradition is the glue that has held the Jewish culture together through millennia of suffering and wandering.

Every family, Jew or Gentile, can apply the principles of the Sabbath. Breaking bread in an unhurried environment adds depth and richness to family relationships. Many families create these occasions a couple of times a year, at Christmas and maybe at a birthday for the matriarch of the family, but for the rest of the year, they rush past one another, believing they're too busy to carve out quality time as a family. The first decision, then, is to make the breaking of bread a priority in the family. Schedule it, prioritize it, and guard it. At least once a week, whether with the extended family or only those who live under your roof, celebrate life together. You may be DINKs (double income, no kids), a single parent with visitation only a couple of days a week, or a family with a host of kids and grandparents living nearby. Whatever the case, come together weekly, and make it something special. Eat gloriously, play games, and engage in rich conversations that welcome give and take. (In other words, listen to your teenagers' views without correcting them!)

I'm not suggesting that one person be responsible for cooking an elaborate spread each week. Part of the joy of being together can be the participation of everyone in the preparation and presentation. Even little children can help set the table and arrange flowers. Perfection isn't the goal; connection and celebration are.

The principles of the Sabbath don't require that we cook traditional Jewish foods. When I visited my family in Israel not long ago, I cooked for them on a Sabbath. I went to the market to buy the freshest ingredients, and I used some recipes that honor our heritage. But you don't have to. Cook what your family loves. Involve others—older family members so they feel honored, and younger ones so they feel valued—overlook little mistakes they make, and enjoy the richness of being together. For some families, not having the television on during meals will take some adjustment. Give people a little time to realize they can actually slow down and enjoy talking with each other when they're eating. Don't force conversation. Take the lead in sharing your heart and asking good questions. Invite them to join the conversation, and sooner or later, they'll feel like talking. Value each person's response even if you disagree, and watch magic happen as people learn to connect with one another in new and meaningful ways.

THE MENU

Mountain Apple Salad with Dijon Vinaigrette

Braised Short Ribs

Passover Vegetable Puffs

Five-Hour Sticky Roast Chicken

Baked Stuffed Apples

Mountain Apple Salad with Dijon Vinaigrette

Serves 4

2 crisp **apples,** cored and sliced
2 cups of **mixed, wild greens**
4 ounces of **Gorgonzola cheese,** crumbled

Caramelized Macadamia Nuts

2 ounces of **butter**
½ cup of **brown sugar**
¾ cup of **macadamia nuts**

Vinaigrette

¼ cup of **sushi vinegar**
2 tablespoons of **whole-grain Dijon mustard**
1 cup of **canola oil**
1 tablespoon of **basil,** chopped
Salt and **pepper** to taste

Garnish

½ cup of **carrot strings**
½ cup of **cucumber strings**

Heat the butter in a sauté pan. Add the brown sugar, and heat until it's melted. Add the macadamia nuts and caramelize them. Allow them to cool on a greased baking sheet.

For the vinaigrette, place the sushi vinegar, basil, and mustard in a blender, and blend on high, slowly adding the oil. Season to taste with salt and pepper.

Mix the wild greens, nuts, and vinaigrette in a large salad bowl. Serve on salad plates, and sprinkle them with Gorgonzola cheese and apple slices.

Garnish with cucumber and carrot strings.

Braised Short Ribs

Serves 8–10

1 bottle of **Cabernet Sauvignon**
2 tablespoons of **vegetable oil**
5 pounds of **short ribs,** trimmed
Salt
1 teaspoon of **black peppercorns,** crushed
Matzo meal, for dredging
10 cloves of **garlic,** peeled
8 large **shallots,** peeled, trimmed, rinsed, split, and dried
2 medium **carrots,** peeled, trimmed, and cut into 1-inch lengths
2 stalks of **celery,** peeled, trimmed, and cut into 1-inch lengths
1 medium **leek,** white and light green parts only, coarsely chopped
6 sprigs of **fresh Italian parsley**
2 sprigs of **fresh thyme**
2 **bay leaves**
2 tablespoons of **tomato paste**
2 quarts of **unsalted beef stock** or **chicken stock**
Freshly ground white pepper

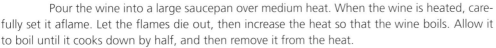

Pour the wine into a large saucepan over medium heat. When the wine is heated, carefully set it aflame. Let the flames die out, then increase the heat so that the wine boils. Allow it to boil until it cooks down by half, and then remove it from the heat.

Center a rack in the oven and preheat the oven to 350.

Heat the oil over medium-high heat in a Dutch oven or a casserole large enough to hold 6 ribs. Season the ribs all over with salt and crushed pepper. Dust the ribs with about 2 tablespoons of matzo meal. When the oil is hot, slip the ribs into the pot and sear them for 4–5 minutes on each side until well-browned.

Transfer the browned ribs to a plate. Remove all but 1 tablespoon of fat from the pot. Lower the heat to medium, and toss in the vegetables and herbs. Brown the vegetables lightly, 5–7 minutes, then stir in the tomato paste and cook for 1 minute to blend everything together.

Add the reduced wine, browned ribs, and stock to the pot. Bring it to a boil, cover the pot tightly, and slide it into the oven to braise for about 2½ hours, or until the ribs are tender enough to be easily pierced with a fork. Every 30 minutes or so, lift the lid to skim off and discard any fat that may have bubbled up to the surface.

Carefully transfer the meat to a heated serving platter with a lip and keep it warm. Boil the pan liquid until it thickens and reduces to approximately 1 quart. Season it with salt and pepper, and pass it through a fine-mesh strainer. Discard the solids.

Pour the sauce over the meat, and serve with vegetables of your choice.

Passover Vegetable Puffs

Serves 10

2 **onions,** chopped

1 pound of **white mushrooms,** chopped

4 tablespoons of **vegetable oil**

40 ounces of **frozen spinach,** thawed and squeezed dry

8 **carrots,** grated

8 **eggs**

1 teaspoon of **salt**

Pepper

4 tablespoons of **chicken soup powder**

1 cup of **matzo meal**

Preheat the oven to 375.

Sauté the onions and mushrooms in a little olive oil. Mix the rest of ingredients together, and add it to the onion/mushroom mixture. Blend well, and spoon the mixture into well-oiled ceramic bowls or muffin tins.

Bake for 40 minutes.

This dish can be frozen. Thaw and warm in a 275-degree oven for 10 minutes.

These puffs can be made in individual muffin tins.

Five-Hour Sticky Roast Chicken

Serves 4

Spice rub

4 teaspoons of **sea salt**
2 teaspoons of **paprika**
1 teaspoon of **onion powder**
1 teaspoon of **cayenne pepper**
1 teaspoon of **thyme**
1 teaspoon of **white pepper**
½ teaspoon of **garlic powder**
½ teaspoon of **black pepper**

Chicken

1 large **roasting chicken**
1 cup of **chopped onion** (for the stuffing)
2 tablespoons of **olive oil**

Thoroughly combine all the ingredients of the spice rub.

Remove all the giblets from the chicken, and clean the cavity well. Wash it and pat dry with paper towels.

Rub the spice mixture into the chicken, both inside and out, making sure it's evenly distributed. Rub it down deep into the skin.

Place the chicken in a re-sealable plastic bag, then seal and refrigerate it overnight.

When you're ready to roast the chicken, preheat the oven to 250. Stuff the cavity of the chicken with onions.

Lightly oil a shallow baking pan. Place the stuffed chicken, breast side up, in the baking pan, and roast it, uncovered, at 250 for 5 hours.

After the first hour, baste the chicken with the pan juices, and continue this process approximately every half hour until the chicken is done. The pan juices will start to caramelize, and the chicken will turn golden brown.

Let the chicken sit about 10 minutes before carving and serving.

Baked Stuffed Apples

Serves 6

6 small **apples**
¼ cup of **golden raisins**
¼ cup of **dark raisins**
2 ounces of **dark rum** (or substitute with **orange juice**)
¼ cup of **walnuts,** chopped
⅓ cup of **honey**
2 tablespoons of **butter**
¼ cup of **confectioner's sugar**
1 cup of **heavy cream**

Preheat the oven to 325.

Butter a baking dish that the apples will fit into snugly. Soak all the raisins in ⅓ cup of the rum for 30 minutes. Peel a wide band of skin from the top of each apple, and use a melon baller to scoop out the core without piercing the bottom.

Stir the nuts and honey into the raisin-rum mixture, and divide the mixture among the apples, pressing it down into each cavity. Top each apple with a teaspoon of butter.

Bake the stuffed apples in the lower part of the 325-degree oven for 30 minutes, basting frequently with the pan juices.

Allow them to cool for 30 minutes. Add the remaining sugar and rum to the cream, and whip into soft peaks. Put a dollop on each apple.

Open House

I've catered open houses for a wide range of occasions, including the opening of new businesses, the presentation of new products, and offering homes or condos for sale. The food and drink at an open house needs to fit the purpose and time of the event. Occasionally, I've been to an open house that was supposed to demonstrate a new product for a company, but the food and drinks were so elaborate that people didn't pay attention to the product. On the other end of the spectrum, I've been to an open house for a new subdivision when the food consisted of a block of cheese and a box of crackers with some canned sodas nearby. The people who came to that event didn't feel they were important enough for the host to provide adequate food and drinks. The results were dismal, but not surprising. Who would buy a $400,000 house from someone who plops a hunk of cheddar and some crackers on a table?

Not long ago, the developers of a vast new housing development asked me to cater an open house for them. I asked them a lot of questions about the people who might be coming to their open house and the tour of model homes, and they told me that they expected people from many different cultures. To make everybody feel honored, we had Mexican food in one model house, Italian in another, and traditional American foods (hamburgers and hot dogs) in another house. The food, drinks, and desserts in each of these appealed to these segments of their client base.

Like every other form of cooking, a little creativity goes a long way to energize the cooks and add spice to the gathering. Whether you are preparing for a formal open house or just having friends over for a relaxed time together, spend some time thinking about the people and the mood you want to create. Prepare the menu and presentation to make it a special time for each person.

Roasted Asparagus Salad with Chèvre

Serves 6

1½ pound of **asparagus**
½ teaspoon of **extra virgin olive oil**
6 **green onions,** chopped
7–8 cups of **mixed baby salad greens**
2 cups of **cherry tomatoes,** red or yellow
¼ pound of **herbed goat cheese** (chèvre),
    cut into 6 slices

Dressing

2 tablespoons of **fresh lemon juice**
4 tablespoons of **light olive oil**
1 tablespoon of **Dijon mustard**
3–4 tablespoons of **chives,** freshly snipped

Preheat the oven to 400. Line a rimmed baking sheet with aluminum foil, and brush it with olive oil.

Snap off any tough ends from the asparagus spears, and trim the breaks with a sharp knife. Using a vegetable peeler and starting just below the tip, peel the skin off each spear down to the end. Arrange the spears in a single layer on the prepared pan, season them with salt and pepper, and drizzle with the extra virgin olive oil. Roast the spears until they are tender, 12–14 minutes. Transfer them to a plate, and set it aside.

For the dressing, whisk together the lemon juice, extra virgin olive oil, and mustard in a small bowl. Stir in the chives, and season the mixture with pepper.

Spoon about 2 tablespoons of the dressing over the asparagus, and let it stand while you toss the salad.

In a large bowl, gently toss together the green onions and the salad greens, and then add the tomatoes. Drizzle just enough of the dressing on the salad so the greens glisten, and then toss again. (You may not use all the dressing.)

Immediately, mound the salad in the center of large, individual salad plates. Place a slice of chèvre on top of each mound of greens, and equally arrange the asparagus spears around the perimeter of each plate.

Drizzle a few extra drops of the remaining dressing over the chèvre, and serve immediately.

Winter Salad with Walnuts, Blue Cheese, and Crostini

Serves 4

1 small head of **radicchio,** with the leaves separated, rinsed, spun dry, and torn into bite size pieces
1 small head of **Boston lettuce,** rinsed, spun dry, and torn into bite-size pieces
1 bunch of **watercress,** rinsed, spun dry, and stems discarded
2 **Belgian endives,** with leaves separated and torn in half

Dressing

1 **shallot,** peeled
2 tablespoons of **sherry vinegar**
½ teaspoon of **kosher salt**
¼ teaspoon of **pepper**
½ cup of **extra virgin olive oil**
¾ teaspoon of **walnut oil**
35 toasted **walnut halves**
½ pound of **blue cheese,** crumbled
Crostini (as an accompaniment)

In a large bowl, toss together the radicchio, the Boston lettuce, the watercress, and the endive.

For the dressing, heat a ridged grill pan over moderately high heat until it's hot but not smoking, and grill the shallots, turning them occasionally, for 5–7 minutes on each side, or until they begin to turn golden and fragrant. Let the shallots cool and finely chop them.

In a bowl, combine the vinegar, salt, pepper, and shallots. Add the oils in a stream, whisking constantly. Whisk the dressing until it's emulsified.

Pour the dressing over the salad, and add the walnuts and blue cheese. Toss the salad to combine it well, and serve it with crostini.

Roasted Beets with Warm Dijon Vinaigrette

Serves 6

3 pounds of medium **beets,** with greens
2 tablespoons of **olive oil**
⅓ cup of **green onions,** sliced
2 tablespoons of **balsamic vinegar**
2 tablespoons of **Dijon mustard**
⅓ cup of **olive oil**
1 teaspoon of **salt,** divided
½ teaspoon of **freshly ground pepper**
1 tablespoon of minced **fresh dill**

Preheat the oven to 400.

Leave the root and 1 inch of the stem on the beets, and reserve the greens. Scrub the beets with a vegetable brush. Drizzle the beets with 1 tablespoon of olive oil, and roast them in a small roasting pan at 400 for 1–1½ hours or until they are tender.

Meanwhile, process the green onions, vinegar, and mustard in a food processor until they are smooth, stopping once to scrape down the sides. With processor running, pour ⅓ cup of olive oil through the food chute, and continue processing until it's smooth. Place the vinegar mixture in a small saucepan, and cook it over low heat until it's thoroughly heated, stirring occasionally.

Wash the beet greens thoroughly, and pat them dry with paper towels. Cut the greens into thin strips.

Place the beet greens in a medium saucepan, cover them with water, and add ½ teaspoon of salt. Bring them to a boil, then reduce the heat and simmer, uncovered, 10 minutes. Drain them well. Set them aside and keep them warm.

Cool the roasted beets. Trim off the roots and stems, and rub off the skins. Cut the beets into ¼-inch slices.

Place the greens and beets on individual servings plates, and top them evenly with the vinegar mixture. Sprinkle with remaining ½ teaspoon of salt, pepper, and dill, and serve immediately.

Citrus-Herb Vinaigrette

1 cup of **orange juice**
½ cup of **lemon juice**
½ cup of **lime juice**
1 tablespoon of **serrano pepper,** minced
2 tablespoons of **dried mint**
2 tablespoons of **dried Thai basil**
2 tablespoons of **dried dill**
2 tablespoons of **dried cilantro**
2 tablespoons of **dried tarragon**

Mix all the ingredients and chill before serving.

Miso Vinaigrette

1 large **egg**
2 teaspoons of **white vinegar**
½ teaspoon of **ginger juice**
¼ teaspoon of **peanut butter**
⅛ teaspoon of **sesame oil**
½ cup of **olive oil**

In a blender, combine the egg, vinegar, and ginger juice. Blend until everything is incorporated, then add the peanut butter, sesame oil, then olive oil until the right consistency is achieved.

Maui Onion Dressing

2 **egg yolks**
1 teaspoon of **garlic,** minced
1 teaspoon of **white pepper**
1 ounce of **Tabasco**
1 ounce of **Worcestershire Sauce**
1 ounce of **fresh lemon juice**
1 teaspoon of **Dijon mustard**
5 cups of **salad oil**
1½ cups of **sugar**
1½ cups of **apple cider vinegar**
2 medium **Maui onions,** chopped

In a bowl, combine the egg yolks, garlic, white pepper, Tabasco, Worcestershire sauce, lemon juice, and mustard. Emulsify the egg yolk mixture and oil together. Add some of the sugar and some of the vinegar intermittently until all the oil, vinegar, and sugar are used up. Finish with the diced onions.

Grilling and Chilling

I enjoy hearing Americans discuss—and often argue about—grilling and barbecuing. They debate the best sauce, vinegar- or tomato-based, and they fiercely defend their preference of chicken, pork, or beef. Those who are dedicated to making the best barbecue of their region, though, cringe when someone says they're going to "barbecue some hamburgers on the grill." Barbecue, the purists insist, always has a rich sauce of one kind or another. Without a sauce, it's just grilling.

Grilling, though, is a high culinary art form.

Whether you grill or barbecue, cooking over hot charcoal or gas is a national pastime millions of us enjoy. Few forms of cooking offer such a variety of ways to prepare so many different meats, fish, and vegetables. You could, with relative ease, cook an entire meal on the grill and enjoy a wonderful blend of flavors. But be careful where you look for advice. Humorist Andy Rooney observed, "Don't take a butcher's advice about how to cook meat. If he knew how, he'd be a chef."

When you grill, consider three distinct elements: the marinade (dry, pastes, or liquid), the way the food is grilled, and the accompaniments. Some of us get locked into grilling only a limited number of foods in a limited range of ways. A little creativity can add new dimensions and rich flavors to cooking over coals or gas.

The place where I live is called The Lofts. To showcase the condos for potential buyers, the managers asked me to cater "The Taste of the Lofts." I prepared a menu that fits the kind of culture and mood the management has created here. We have six swimming pools, so we created the theme of "Grilling and Chilling," and we set up our stations at each of the pools. We had a variety of grilled foods and accompaniments. The most popular station was where we served Bananas Foster-esque splits.

Sirloin Steak

1-inch or 2-inch thick cuts of **steak**

Rub the meat lightly with garlic-marinated olive oil. I prefer a dry rub: Clive's, a Montréal seasoning, or just a clove of garlic and then seasoned with salt and pepper.

Cut the fat vertically at 1-inch intervals.

Start cooking over high heat for 1 minute, then turn the steak 45 degrees and cook for another minute. Turn the steak over (using tongs, not a fork) and repeat the same process. Turn the grill to low (or use another section of the grill that's on low) and cook with the lid covered for 3–5 minutes.

Allow the steak to rest for 5 minutes. Season to taste with finishing sea salt before slicing and serving.

Beef Tenderloin

2-inch center cut **fillets**, about 8 ounces each (The end pieces of the tenderloin, which are accurately called Filet Mignon, can be used in sautéed ragouts and quick stews.)

Because this cut of meat already is tender and flavorful, there's no need to marinate; just season it a bit with sea salt and cracked black pepper.

If you are grilling, lightly coat the meat with olive oil, and then season with salt and pepper. Add a little cocoa or ground coffee into the rub for an extra dimension of flavor.

Start cooking on the medium/high part of the grill for 1 minute, then turn it 45 degrees for 1 minute longer. Move it to medium/low heat and cook to the desired doneness (I recommend medium rare, 140 degrees). It's best to cook the steak for the last 3–5 minutes on the raised part of the grill (if you have it).

Allow it to rest for 5 minutes before serving.

Whole tenderloin can be marinated the same way as tenderloin steaks. For an average 4-pound tenderloin, cook it approximately 25 minutes so it's medium rare. Start cooking on medium-high heat until entire outside has been seared. Baste regularly, and cook on low-medium heat until desired doneness. If the end (mignon) is over 160, the center should be rare.

Allow it to rest for 5 minutes before slicing and serving.

RECIPES

Sirloin Steak

Beef Tenderloin

Ribeye Steak

Chicken Breasts

Baked Potatoes

Relishes and Marinade

Perfect Sides

Ribeye Steak

18- to 20-ounce **steaks,** trimmed of excess side fat

Wet and dry marinades work well with ribeyes (see marinade recipes).

Before cooking, wipe the excess marinade from the meat.

Over medium heat, sear the steaks for 1 minute, then turn them 45 degrees for another minute. Repeat on other side, and finish cooking at a lower heat (approximately 4 minutes for medium rare).

Allow steaks to rest for 3 minutes. They can be sliced when they are served.

Chicken Breasts

Boneless, 10- to 12-ounce **chicken breasts**

Place the breasts between parchment papers, and pound them with a mallet to make the meat uniform before marinating and cooking.

The marinades you choose can range from dry to highly flavored wet ones.

Place the breasts (skin side down if you leave the skin on) on high heat for 1 minute, then turn them 45 degrees and cook them for another minute. Turn them over and repeat the cooking times. Move to medium heat and cook for 8 more minutes, turning and basting with marinade 2–3 times. Cook until the center of the meat reaches 150 degrees.

Allow the breasts to rest 3 minutes before you slice and serve.

10 Commandments of Baked Potatoes

1. Choose potatoes with uniform size that have no wrinkles or sprouts.

2. Prick potatoes with a fork to shorten the baking time.

3. Wash potatoes thoroughly with a vegetable brush and dry them well.

4. Don't wrap potatoes in aluminum foil for baking. Foil holds in moisture and steams the potatoes, resulting in a "boiled" taste and texture.

5. Pour enough rock salt into a baking pan to cover the bottom.

6. Arrange the potatoes on top of the salt layer with a bit of space between them.

7. Bake at 400 for about one hour.

8. A baked potato is ready when a fork easily pierces its skin. If the potato is hard, bake it a little longer.

9. Allow potatoes to rest for 5 minutes, then lift each potato out with tongs. Brush away any salt that may have stuck to the potato skin.

10. Serve with butter, sour cream, and freshly snipped chives. Eat the skins, too!

"Potatoes, like wives, should never be taken for granted." —Peter Pirbright

Relishes and Marinade for Grilled Foods

Here are some of my favorites...

Avocado Pico de Gallo

2 **Roma tomatoes,** peeled, cored, and seeded
1 **serrano pepper,** with the stem, vein, and seeds removed, minced
4 tablespoons of **cilantro leaves,** roughly chopped
¾ teaspoon of **salt**
1 teaspoon of **freshly ground pepper**
1 **avocado,** cut in 1-inch pieces
1 tablespoon of **fresh lime juice**

Dice the tomatoes into ⅜-inch cubes, and transfer them to a medium bowl. Add the serrano pepper, cilantro, salt, pepper, avocado, and lime juice. Toss the ingredients well to combine them, and set it aside for 30 minutes to enhance the flavors.

Mustard Mint Sauce

Serve with grilled salmon.

6 tablespoons of **Dijon mustard**
6 tablespoons of **grain mustard**
3 ounces of **rice wine vinegar**
1 cup of **mint leaves,** chopped
1 cup of **olive oil**
½ cup of **honey**

Blend all the ingredients together.

Cranberry Chutney Sauce

1 1-pound bag of **cranberries**
½ cup of **celery,** chopped
½ cup of **onion,** chopped
The zest of 2 **oranges**
¼ cup of **brown sugar**
½ cup of **sugar**
1 teaspoon of **ground cloves**
1 **cinnamon stick**
½ cup of **golden raisins**
1½ cups of **water**
1 cup of **red wine**

Mix all the ingredients and bring them to a boil. Cook for 45 minutes on medium heat, stirring often. Allow the mixture to sit for 24 hours in the refrigerator before serving—and be sure to take the cinnamon stick out before serving.

Pear-Honey Chutney

8 **pears,** peeled and diced into 1-inch pieces
½ cup of **honey**
¾ cup of **lemon juice,** plus the zest of 1 **lemon**
½ cup of **cider vinegar**
¼ cup of **apple cider**
¼ teaspoon of **grated ginger**
¼ teaspoon of **cayenne pepper**
1 **yellow bell pepper,** minced
½ of a small **onion,** chopped
½ cup of **raisins**
Salt to taste

Bring all the ingredients to a boil, then turn the heat to medium and let them simmer in the saucepan until the pears are tender (about 30 minutes). Cool to room temperature and refrigerate.

Black Bean and Pepper Relish

½ of a **yellow bell pepper,** diced in ¼-inch pieces
½ of a **red bell pepper,** diced in ¼-inch pieces
1 cup of cooked **black beans**
2 tablespoons of **olive oil**
1 clove of **garlic,** minced
1 **shallot,** chopped
¼ cup of **rice wine vinegar**
1 tablespoon of **maple syrup**
2 tablespoons of **fresh cilantro,** minced
Salt and **pepper**

Put the peppers and black beans in a shallow dish.

Heat the olive oil in a small skillet over medium heat. Add the garlic and shallot, and cook until they're soft, about 2 minutes.

Add the vinegar and maple syrup, and remove the pan from the heat. Pour the mixture over the peppers and beans, add the cilantro, and mix gently.

Season to taste with salt and pepper. Refrigerate the relish at least 2 hours, stirring it several times to coat the ingredients in the dressing.

Black-Eyed Pea Relish

1 cup of **dried black-eyed peas**

1 small **sweet potato,** peeled and diced into ½-inch pieces

¼ cup of **extra virgin olive oil**

4 medium **sweet onions,** minced

¼ cup of **red bell pepper,** minced

¼ cup of **flat leaf parsley,** minced

2 tablespoons of **fresh basil,** minced

2 tablespoons of **chives,** minced

2 tablespoons of **raspberry vinegar**

Salt and **freshly cracked pepper**

In a bowl, cover the black-eyed peas with warm water, and let them soak for 1 hour. Drain and rinse them carefully to remove any dirt, and then drain them again.

Place the black-eyed peas in a saucepan, and add enough water to cover them by 1 inch. Add the sweet potato and a dash of salt, and bring them to a boil over high heat. Reduce the heat to low, and simmer gently until the peas and potatoes are tender (15–20 minutes). Drain them and set them aside.

In a large skillet, heat the olive oil over moderate heat. Add the onions and cook them, stirring often, until they are translucent (about 7 minutes). Set them aside to cool. Stir in the red bell pepper, parsley, basil, chives, vinegar, peas, and potatoes, and season with pepper. Serve at room temperature. (Shown at right served with London Broil.)

London Broil Marinade

1 cup of **soy sauce**
½ cup of **brown sugar**
½ cup of **red wine vinegar**
½ cup of **pineapple juice**
2 teaspoons of **salt**
1 tablespoon of **fresh thyme**
½ teaspoon of **garlic powder**
½ cup of **sweet Texas red wine**
¼ cup of **olive oil**

Mix all the ingredients and marinate the meat overnight for your choice of grilling. Cook the meat over charcoal or mesquite wood.

The Perfect Sides for Grilled Food
Wild Mushroom Ragout in Flaky Pastry

Serves 4

1 sheet of **puff pastry**
2 **eggs**
2 teaspoons of **water**
1 pound of **assorted mushrooms**
4 tablespoons of **butter**
2 **shallots,** chopped
4 tablespoons of **cognac**
2 cups of **heavy cream**
2 tablespoons of **foie gras**

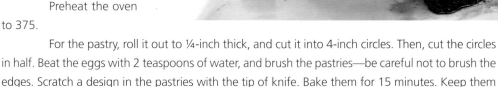

Preheat the oven to 375.

For the pastry, roll it out to ¼-inch thick, and cut it into 4-inch circles. Then, cut the circles in half. Beat the eggs with 2 teaspoons of water, and brush the pastries—be careful not to brush the edges. Scratch a design in the pastries with the tip of knife. Bake them for 15 minutes. Keep them warm until the dish is ready to serve.

For the ragout, clean the mushrooms and slice them. Melt the butter in a small casserole dish. Add the shallots, and cook them until they're soft. Add the mushrooms, season them, and cook them, covered, for 4 minutes. Deglaze with the cognac. Bring the mixture to a boil. Add the cream, and cook the mixture over low heat until it's reduce by half. Before serving, press the foie gras through a fine sieve, and stir it into the sauce.

Open the pastry shells, fill them with the ragout mixture, and serve immediately.

Lemon and Thyme Potato Gratin

Serves 4

2 tablespoons of **unsalted butter,** plus some extra melted butter for the pan
2 pounds of **Yukon Gold potatoes,** peeled and sliced very thin
2 teaspoons of **fresh thyme leaves,** chopped
⅛ teaspoon of **freshly grated nutmeg**
The zest of 1 **lemon,** finely chopped (about 2 teaspoons)
½ cup of **milk**
Salt and **freshly ground pepper**

Preheat the oven to 400.

Place a baking sheet on the lower rack. Brush a 10 x 5½-inch gratin dish with melted butter. Cover the bottom of the gratin dish with ⅓ of the potato slices in an even layer. Sprinkle the potatoes with ⅓ of the thyme, nutmeg, and lemon zest, and season to taste with salt and pepper. Dot this layer with butter.

Add a second layer, and season it the same way. Add a third layer of potato slices arranged neatly, and pour the milk over the potatoes. Sprinkle with the remaining third of thyme, nutmeg, and lemon zest. Dot the top with butter, and season to taste with salt and pepper. Cover the dish with foil.

Bake for 40 minutes, then remove the foil, and continue to bake for 10–20 minutes, until the top is golden brown and the potatoes are tender when they're pierced with the tip of a knife.

Potato Pancake

Serves 4

3 large **golden potatoes**
6 tablespoons of **unsalted butter**
3 **shallots,** finely chopped
Salt and **pepper** to taste

Preheat the oven to 450.

Cut the potatoes in thin, round slices (⅛-inch). Use a mandolin if you have one.

Melt ½ of the butter in an omelette pan, and lightly caramalize the shallots. Remove the shallots and add the rest of the butter to the pan.

Layer the potato slices around the pan so that they completely cover the bottom of the pan. Make another layer of potato slices.

Place the shallots in the middle of the potatoes. Continue building 2 more layers of potatoes until all the potatoes are in the pan. Brush each layer with butter in the pan.

On medium heat, cook the bottom part of the pancake for 3–4 minutes—be careful not to let it burn.

Take the pan off the stove and bake it at 450 until golden brown, 20–25 minutes. Allow the pancake to cool slightly before cutting it into wedges.

Shallot Spoon Bread

Serves 8

¾ cup of melted **butter**
1 cup of **sour cream**
1 cup of **fresh corn** (optional)
½ cup of **shallots,** diced and caramelized
¾ cup of **creamed corn,** puréed in a blender
1 box (3 cups) of **corn bread mix**

Preheat the oven to 350.

Spray a casserole dish with 4-inch sides with quick release cooking spray. First incorporate all the wet ingredients, including the corn and shallots, followed by the corn bread mix.

Bake at 350 for 30–45 minutes or until the cake springs back when touched.

Eggplant Casserole

Serves 12

4 medium **eggplants**
2 pounds of **sausage**
2 cans of **tomatoes with green chilies**
8 ounces of **mushrooms,** washed and sliced
1 medium **yellow onion,** chopped
1 stick of **butter**
2 cups of **Italian breadcrumbs**
3½ cups of **cheddar cheese**
1½ cups of **grated Parmesan cheese**
½ teaspoon of **salt**
Black pepper to taste (I use about 2 teaspoons)

Preheat the oven to 400.

Cut the eggplants in half. Remove the eggplant from the skin in small pieces, leaving the skin intact. Boil the eggplant in water with ½ teaspoon of salt until it's tender (about 15 minutes).

While the eggplant is boiling, crumble the sausage into a skillet and cook it. Drain the grease and set the sausage aside. Wipe the skillet with a paper towel, and add the butter to the pan. Melt the butter on low heat, add the mushrooms and chopped onions, and cook them at low heat until the onions are translucent.

Drain the eggplant. Add the cooked sausage, vegetables, tomatoes with green chilies, cheddar cheese, breadcrumbs, and pepper to the eggplant. Mix well, then add 1¼ cups of Parmesan cheese to the mixture. Save the rest of the Parmesan.

Spoon the eggplant mixture into the skins and bake for 30 minutes at 400. Remove them and sprinkle the remaining Parmesan cheese on top. Then bake them for another 5 minutes. When serving, spoon the eggplant from the shells.

Leftovers freeze well and can be easily reheated.

Warm Potato Salad

Serves 6–8

1 pint of **vegetable broth** or **water**
4 cloves of **garlic,** divided
1 sprig of **fresh rosemary**
1 sprig of **fresh thyme**
1 **bay leaf**
3 pounds of **potatoes,** cut into 1½-inch pieces
¼ pound (about 5 slices) of **bacon,** cut into 1-inch pieces
2 **shallots,** cut into thin slices
1 tablespoon of **sherry vinegar**
4 ounces (about 4 cups) of **frisée,** washed
1½ teaspoons of **salt,** divided
¾ teaspoon of **pepper,** divided

In large saucepan, bring the broth, 3 cloves of garlic, rosemary, thyme, and bay leaf to a boil over medium-high heat. Add the potatoes and boil uncovered for 10–13 minutes, or until the potatoes are just tender. Drain the potatoes, discarding the herb sprigs and garlic cloves, then set the potatoes aside.

In a large, non-stick skillet, cook the bacon over medium heat for 8–10 minutes, or until it's crisp. Drain the bacon on paper towels, and reserve the bacon fat. In the same skillet, cook and stir the potatoes in the reserved bacon fat for 6–8 minutes, or until they're golden brown. Mince the remaining clove of garlic. Add the garlic and shallots to the potato mixture, and cook it for 2–3 minutes, or until the shallots are soft, stirring often. Add the reserved, cooked bacon and vinegar, mixing until everything is combined.

Whipped Sweet Potatoes

Serves 8

3 pounds of **sweet potatoes,** peeled and cut in 2-inch cubes
4 cups of **apple cider**
3 cups of **water**
The peel of an **orange**
1 **cinnamon stick**
1 **bay leaf**
1 **onion** studded with **cloves**
2 ounces of **butter**
1 **Golden Delicious apple,** diced
1 **banana,** sliced
¼ cup of **sugar**
The juice of 1 **orange**
1 cup of **heavy cream**

Boil the sweet potatoes in water and cider with the orange peel, cinnamon stick, bay leaf, and an onion studded with cloves. Cook for 20–25 minutes.

Melt the butter in a pan. Add the banana, apple, and sugar, and caramelize them about 4 minutes. Add the orange juice, and bring it to a gentle boil for 2 minutes.

Add the heavy cream to the mixture, and bring it to a boil for 5 minutes.

Remove the cinnamon stick and the orange peel. Add the potatoes to the mixture, and purée them in small batches in a food processor, adding cream to thin it if necessary—don't over-process it.

The potatoes can be made a day ahead and refrigerated. Reheat them in a buttered baking dish at 350 for 25 minutes.

Garnish with dried cranberries sautéed in butter.

Yorkshire Pudding

Serves 6

¾ cup of **all-purpose flour**
½ teaspoon of **salt**
2 **eggs**
1 cup of **milk**
4 tablespoons of **vegetable oil**

Beat the flour, salt, eggs, and milk together until it's very smooth, scraping the bowl occasionally. Refrigerate 2 hours or longer.

Preheat the oven to 450.

Measure the oil into an 8 x 8 x 2-inch square Pyrex pan. Heat it in the oven for 2 minutes. Pour the batter into the pan, and bake it for 20–30 minutes—don't open the door! Serve immediately.

When it's fresh from the oven, good Yorkshire pudding is a puffy, irregular shaped golden mass, unlike any other baked dish. After standing a few minutes, the surface settles more or less evenly. When it's cut, the outer crust is tender and crisp, and the center is soft like custard.

Can also be baked in muffin tins.

Christmas Dinner

Sadly, I think many families miss the point of Christmas. We get caught up in the commercialism of the season, and we make the event about presents (and increasingly more expensive presents) instead of the One whose birth we celebrate. Many families try to combine the spiritual and the material, but the avalanche of advertising and the anticipation of gifts often overwhelm the real message. I suggest we come at it from a fresh, very different perspective.

Rigorously guard the true meaning of Christmas. Block out as much of the focus on gifts as you can. Replace those expectations with a powerful blend of the simple and the majestic. Think about the simplicity of a couple having a baby in the most humble place imaginable, while around them, the heavens rang with angels singing praises to this tiny baby. Push away the crass commercialism of the season by opening presents at a different time than your family celebrates Christ's birth. In our culture, we've made gift-giving central to the day, but we need to remember that the only people present on the day of Jesus' birth were his parents, a few shepherds who had heard the angels sing, and Jesus. The wise men came with their gifts at a later time. The focus on gifts, I believe very strongly, detracts from the powerful significance that the eternal God became human to touch our lives.

Since this is the only time (or one of the only times) of the year that many families get together, they often make it a massive production. The burden of preparation often falls on one or a few people, and these few can become so frazzled and exhausted that they can't reflect on the real meaning of Christmas and can't enjoy the people they serve. Instead, make gathering together a more frequent event (see the section on the Sabbath) and make the Christmas event far simpler. My tradition is to serve tamales and gumbo—nothing more and nothing else. Involve others, including children and teenagers, in the preparation. Don't get caught up in an elaborate, time-consuming, exhausting production. Keep it simple, meaningful, and fun. Create a new, richer tradition for your family.

Rio Bravo Tamales

Makes about 2 dozen tamales

4 cups of freshly cooked **chicken** in
    1-inch cubes
12 cups of **basic masa**
24 **dried cornhusks,** soaked, washed,
    and drained, plus more for ties
Chicken Sauce

Chicken Sauce

1 16-ounce can of **whole tomatoes**
4 tablespoons of **olive oil**
2 meduim **onions,** chopped
2 **serrano peppers,** minced
1 teaspoon of **dried oregano**
1 teaspoon of **ground cumin**
1 teaspoon of **sea salt**
1 teaspoon of **freshly ground
    black pepper**

Prepare the masa.

To make the sauce, drain the tomatoes (reserving the liquid), Coarsely chop them and set them aside. Heat the oil in a skillet over medium heat. Sauté the onions for 2–3 minutes, until they're soft. Add the peppers, oregano, cumin, salt, and pepper, and cook for 1–2 minutes, until the onions are translucent and the flavors are incorporated. Add the tomatoes and the reserved liquid, and simmer for 20 minutes, until the tomatoes are soft and beginning to break down. Remove the mixture from the heat, and let it cool to room temperature. Fold the chicken into the sauce, and set it aside.

To assemble the tamales, spread ½ cup of masa across the center of the smooth side of each cornhusk. Place 1 heaping tablespoon of the chicken mixture in the center of the masa, and fold both sides over the filling. Tie both ends of the tamale while squeezing in the ends to make it plump. Prick the tamale several times with a knife to create vent holes. Repeat this process for the remaining tamales. Steam the tamales for 1 hour or until done.

Basic Masa

1 cup of **chicken stock***
2/3 cup of **white grits,** finely ground, or **white cornmeal**
1 cup of **masa harina**
1/3 cup of **whole milk yogurt cheese***
1 teaspoon of **baking powder**
1/2–1 teaspoon of **salt**

To make yogurt cheese, pour plain yogurt into a sieve lined with cheese cloth. Set over a bowl and let drain for 4 hours.

When the cheese is ready, bring stock to a simmer, then pour over grits in a bowl and allow to soften for about 15 minutes.

Mix in masa harina; set aside until cool. In a mixer fitted with a whisk attachment, or with an electric hand mixer, combine half the masa mixture and yogurt, beating for three minutes. Add remaining masa and mix another 3 minutes, to the consistency of cake batter. Add baking powder and salt to taste.

*Allergy notes: If you are allergic to soy, be sure the broth you choose is soy-free, as broths frequently contain hydrolized vegetable protein from soy. The egg protein lysozyme is an unlabeled additive in some cheeses. People allergic to eggs should eliminate any cheese in this recipe.

RECIPES

Rio Bravo Tamales

Maureen's Cabbage Soup

The Best Turkey
Dressing Ever

Brisket of Beef
with Pears and Prunes

Zucchini Bread

Pecan Puffs

Maureen's Cabbage Soup

Serves 6–8 as a main course

2 pounds of **short ribs**
1 large **cabbage,** shredded
1 28-ounce can of **chopped tomatoes**
1 14-ounce can of **tomato purée**
1 large **onion,** chopped
6 cups of **chicken broth**
1 tablespoon of **salt**
½ teaspoon of **cracked black pepper**
⅓ cup of **light brown sugar**
2 tablespoons of **lemon juice**

Place the meat in a large soup pot, cover with water, and boil over medium heat for ½ hour. Remove the meat from the water, and set it aside.

Drain the water, and fill the soup pot with the remaining ingredients. Cover and bring to a boil. Simmer for 20 minutes. Add the meatballs and short ribs and simmer for another 10 minutes.

Meatballs

1 small **onion,** chopped
1 pound of **lean ground beef or veal**
1 tablespoon of **plain breadcrumbs**
1 teaspoon of **chicken broth powder** (or crushed bouillon cube)
1 chopped, ripe **tomato,** skinned and seeds removed
1 **Granny Smith apple,** grated
A pinch of **ground ginger**
1 **egg,** beaten
2 quarts of **chicken stock**

Mix all the ingredients together, roll into small balls, and place them in boiling chicken stock for 10 minutes. Then add the meatballs to the soup.

The Best Turkey Dressing Ever

To stuff an 8–10 pound turkey

1 cup of **raisins**
1 cup of **Marsala**
1 pound of **sausage**
1 cup of **carrots,** shredded
1 cup of **celery,** chopped
½ cup of **onions,** chopped
½ cup of **margarine, butter,** or **olive oil**
¼ teaspoon of **ground nutmeg**
¼ teaspoon of **sea salt**
¼ teaspoon of **black pepper**
8 cups of **dry bread cubes** (or less if you prefer)
2 cups of **apples,** peeled and finely chopped (Granny Smith is
    best)
½ cup of chopped **walnuts** (roasted and crunchy)
¼ cup of **toasted wheat germ**
½–1 cup of **chicken broth**

Marinate the raisins in Marsala the night before.

Sauté the sausage, and drain off the grease.

In a large skillet, cook the carrots, celery, and onion in margarine, butter, or olive oil until they're tender. Stir in the nutmeg, salt, and pepper.

In a bowl, combine the bread cubes, apple, walnuts, and wheat germ. Add the carrot mixture, raisins, and sausage. Drizzle with enough broth to moisten the mixture, and toss lightly. Stuff the turkey and bake.

Brisket of Beef
with Pears and Prunes

Serves 8

5 pounds of **brisket**
Salt and **pepper**
1 teaspoon of **ginger**
¼ cup of **vegetable oil**
2 large **onions,** chopped
2 cloves of **garlic**
1 cup of **beef stock**
¼ cup of **lemon juice**
¼ cup of **brown sugar**
¼ cup of **Lyle's Golden Syrup**
8 **potatoes,** peeled and cut into quarters
2 **yams,** peeled and cut into quarters
4 **carrots,** peeled and sliced
6 firm **pears,** unpeeled
½ pound of **prunes**

Preheat the oven to 350. In a large roasting pan, sprinkle the meat liberally with salt, pepper, and ginger. Brown the meat in hot oil. Add the onions, and brown slightly.

Place the brisket, onions, garlic, and stock in the pan, cover, and roast it for 2½ hours. Add extra stock or boiling water when necessary.

Add lemon juice, brown sugar, and syrup, and cook for another 15 minutes. Add potatoes, yams, carrots, whole pears, and prunes, and cook another hour before serving.

Note: The potatoes, yams, and pears should be cut in 1-inch pieces.

Zucchini Bread

4 **eggs**
1¼ cups of **vegetable oil**
2 cups of **sugar**
1 teaspoon of **vanilla**
2½ cups of grated **zucchini**
2½ cups of **all-purpose flour**
2 teaspoons of **baking soda**
2 teaspoons of **baking powder**
1 teaspoon of **salt**
1 teaspoon of **cinnamon**
1 teaspoon of **ground cloves**
1 cup of **walnuts,** chopped

Preheat the oven to 350. Mix all the ingredients in large bowl.
Butter a small loaf pan. Bake until firm to touch (a tooth pick comes out clean).
Zucchini bread is a perfect accompaniment to paté or salad.

Pecan Puffs

The best cookie I have ever had!

Makes 20

¼ pound of **butter**
2 tablespoons of **sugar**
1 tablespoon of **vanilla extract**
1 cup of **pecans** (or walnuts for Walnut Puffs), ground in a food processor
1 cup of **all-purpose flour**
1 cup of **confectioner's sugar**

Preheat the oven to 300.
Cream the butter and sugar. Add the remaining ingredients (except for the confectioner's sugar) to make the dough.
Roll the dough into small balls, and place them on greased baking sheets in the freezer until they are thoroughly chilled.
Bake the balls for about 40 minutes. While they are still hot, roll the puffs in powdered sugar. Then, when they have cooled, roll them again in powdered sugar.

Super Bowl

Every city in America has its own culture and cuisine, so when you find out which two teams are playing in the Super Bowl, do some research to discover the unique foods and drink that represent each city. Not long ago, the two teams in the championship were from New York (the Giants) and Boston (the New England Patriots). Both of these cities are rich in indigenous foods. For our party, we served crab cakes, Buffalo wings, hot dogs, clam chowder, chicken tenders, and cheesecake. It was perfect for the game.

If one of the teams is from a fairly unimaginative city (Cleveland comes to mind), you might have to be a bit creative, but most cities are known for their unique local foods and restaurants.

Salmon Tart

Serves 4 as an appetizer

4 6-inch rounds of **puff pastry**
8 ounces of fresh, skinned **salmon**
4 tablespoons of **cream cheese**
1 tablespoon of **fresh dill,** chopped
2 tablespoons of **red onions,** chopped
2 tablespoons of melted **butter**
Seasoning salt

Preheat the oven to 375.

Brush the pastry with egg wash, and dock with a fork. Bake the rounds until they're a light golden color.

Mix the cream cheese, dill, onions, and seasoning salt. Let the mixture stand at room temperature so it can soften.

Spread the cream cheese mixture over each pastry round. Slice the salmon in thin pieces, and place them over the cream cheese.

Brush each one with melted butter, and place them under a broiler until they're done (about 2–3 minutes).

Serve with lemon butter sauce, using the recipe for Beurre Blanc on page 115, and adding the zest of ½ a lemon and ½ teaspoon lemon juice after the sauce has been strained.

RECIPES

Salmon Tart

Oriental Dipping Sauce

Caribbean Dipping Sauce

Honey Mustard
Dipping Sauce

Pesto Dipping Sauce

Blue Cheese Dip

Sweet Onion, Bean,
& Artichoke Dip

In addition to the dishes that are indigenous to the cities represented by Super Bowl teams, great dips go with everything. Here are my favorites.

Oriental Dipping Sauce

½ cup of **mayonnaise**
3 tablespoons of **Worcestershire sauce**
2 tablespoons of **olive oil**
2 tablespoons of **oriental sesame oil**
1½ tablespoons of **honey**
1 tablespoon of **fresh lemon juice**
¾ teaspoon of **seasoning salt**

Mix well and serve with chips, toasted pita bread, or toasted French bread.

Caribbean Dipping Sauce

½ cup of **plain yogurt,** drained in cheesecloth
½ cup of **mayonnaise**
½ cup of **mango chutney,** drained and chopped
1 teaspoon of **fresh lime juice**
2 teaspoons of **curry powder,** toasted
2 tablespoons of minced **red onion**
¼ teaspoon of **cayenne pepper,** toasted

Mix well.

Honey Mustard Dipping Sauce

Serves 10

1 cup of **Dijon mustard**
½ cup of **sour cream**
½ cup of **mayonnaise**
½ cup of **honey**
½ teaspoon of **seasoning salt**
⅛ teaspoon of **Worcestershire sauce**

In a bowl, mix the mayonnaise and sour cream until it's smooth. Add the mustard and honey, and mix well. Finally, add seasoning salt and Worcestershire sauce, and mix well. Serve this dipping sauce cold.

Pesto Dipping Sauce

Serves 8

1 cup of **fresh basil leaves**
1 cup of **Parmesan cheese**
3¼ ounces of **pine nuts,** toasted
1 cup of **olive oil**
¼ teaspoon of **salt**

In a food processor, mix all the ingredients together until it's smooth. (Or you can use a hand mixer and a bowl.)

Blue Cheese Dip

Serves 8

1 cup of **blue cheese**
1 cup of **sour cream**
1 cup of **mayonnaise**
Salt and **lemon pepper**

Mix all the ingredients together and serve.

Sweet Onion, Bean, & Artichoke Dip

Serves 6

2 tablespoons of **olive oil**
1 cup of **Vidalia** (or **Texas 1015**) **onion,** chopped
2 teaspoons of **sugar**
4 cloves of **garlic,** chopped
1 15-ounce can of **cannellini beans,** drained
1 tablespoon of **fresh oregano,** chopped
1 tablespoon of **fresh tarragon,** chopped
1 tablespoon of **lemon juice**
1 12-ounce jar of **marinated artichokes,** drained
Cayenne pepper to taste
Salt and **pepper** to taste

Heat the oil over medium-high heat and add the onion, sugar, and garlic. Turn the heat to medium, and cook about 20 minutes until the onion is golden brown—don't let it burn. Combine the onion mixture with the remaining ingredients in a food processor, and blend until it's smooth.

Taking the "Wild" out of Game

If you're a hunter, the spouse of a hunter, or just someone who loves the taste of wild game, you can do a few simple things to enhance the flavor and keep it from overpowering everything else in the meal. For venison, I use buttermilk with a light seasoning because it has a lower acidity and prevents the meat from tasting too gamey. You can also marinate the meat in a light brine solution. Game typically needs strong sauces and side dishes to balance or mask the potent flavor. I often use polenta or wild rice as sides. Some vegetables don't usually work well because their flavors are too delicate. Use root vegetables, such as beets, Brussel sprouts, turnips, and celeriac. Unlike meats we buy at the store, wild game is very lean, so we need to use larger amounts of fat in the cooking.

The most common mistake people make when preparing game is to marinate it in something, such as vinegar, wine, and lemon juice, that actually enhances the gamey flavor. And the most common mistake in cooking it is overcooking, which makes a lean piece of meat even dryer and robs it of flavor and tenderness.

I know a few people who are masters at preparing wild game for their families and friends. Cooking game requires a deft touch, or the results can be inedible. A good marinade, adding fat when cooking, and bringing it to the right temperature, though, can result in a dish everyone can enjoy.

Spicy Game Seasoning

½ cup of **paprika**
½ cup of **sea salt**
½ cup of **ground black pepper**
½ cup of **garlic powder**
6 tablespoons of **onion powder**
4 tablespoons of **cayenne pepper**
4 tablespoons of **oregano**
2 tablespoons of **ground white pepper**

Mix all the ingredients together, and sprinkle the seasoning over all the game before cooking.

Venison Stew

Serve over mashed sweet or savory potatoes, or a wild rice blend.

Serves 4–6

½ pound of sliced **bacon,** cut into rough pieces

2 pounds of **venison stew meat,** cut in 1-inch cubes

All-purpose flour seasoned with **salt, pepper,** and
    paprika

1 cup of **light red wine**

1 medium **white onion,** sliced

2 small **carrots,** roughly chopped

2 cloves of **garlic,** minced

1 tablespoon of **Worcestershire sauce**

1 bay leaf

½ teaspoon of **dried thyme**

1 teaspoon of **sea salt**

2 cups of **beef stock** mixed with 1 cup of **water**

2 tablespoons of **butter** and 2 tablespoons of **all-purpose flour**
    mixed together at room temperature (if necessary)

Cook the bacon until it's lightly crisp, and then remove it from the pan.

Dredge the meat in the seasoned flour. Pour the bacon fat into a large pot on medium-high heat, add the venison (half at a time) and cook until golden brown on all sides. Add the wine, and stir well, scraping the bottom until the wine has reduced by half.

Stir in the onion, carrots, garlic, Worcestershire sauce, bay leaf, thyme, salt, and beef stock. Reduce the heat to medium-low, cover the pan, and cook it for 1½–2 hours, or until the meat is tender.

Adjust the seasoning and the consistency. If it's too thin, mix 2 tablespoons of butter with 2 tablespoons of flour, stir it into stew, and bring it to a boil.

Garnish with chopped bacon and parsley.

RECIPES

Spicy Game Seasoning

Venison Stew

*South Texas Quail...
with an Italian Twist*

*Roast Duck
with Minted Orange*

South Texas Quail...
with an Italian Twist

Serves 4

4 **whole quail,** deboned
3 ounces of **olive oil**
2 tablespoons of **fresh sage,** chopped
2 cloves of **garlic,** chopped
4 pieces of **apple-smoked bacon**

Sauce

1 small **tomato,** diced
3 tablespoons of toasted **pine nuts**
3 ounces of **unsalted butter**
2 cloves of **garlic,** minced
The juice of half a **lemon**
4 ounces of **dry vermouth** (white wine will work)

Mix the olive oil, sage, and garlic to form a paste.

Season the quail with salt and white pepper, then rub it with the herb paste inside and out. Marinate for at least 4 hours in the refrigerator.

Preheat the oven to 300.

Allow the quail to come to room temperature. Heat the olive oil in a thick-bottom skillet on top of the stove and add the quail. Brown them lightly on all sides, allow them to cool, and then wrap each quail with a small piece of bacon. Place them in a roasting pan.

Roast the quail for 5–7 minutes, and then remove them from the pan and allow them to rest. Drain oil from the pan, add vermouth and garlic, and reduce by a third.

Add pine nuts, lemon juice, and tomatoes. Reduce until the desired flavor and a thick consistency is reached. Season with salt and pepper.

Serve the quail on a bed of creamed polenta or risotto, and cover them with the sauce.

Roast Duck with Minted Oranges

Serves 4

2 **whole boneless Moulard duck breasts,** halved and trimmed
4 **Minted Oranges**
1 tablespoon of **cumin**
1 tablespoon of **nutmeg**
1 tablespoon of **cinnamon**
1 tablespoon of **ground cloves**
1 tablespoon of **coriander**
The juice of 1 **lemon** and 1 **orange**
¼ cup of **honey**

Grind all the spices together and season the duck breasts. Mix the orange and lemon juice with the honey. Place the duck breasts in the honey marinade for 3–5 hours, turning twice.

Minted Oranges

4 **oranges,** peeled
½ cup of **sugar**
1 cup of **water**
2 tablespoons of **Grand Marnier**
2 tablespoons of **white crème de menthe**
6 **mint leaves,** chopped

Sauce

½ cup of **orange juice**
¼ cup of **honey**

To make the Minted Oranges, bring all the ingredients to a boil, and reduce by half. Add the peeled oranges, and remove it from the stove to chill. The oranges may also be served as a dessert.

After the duck breasts have fully marinated, make the sauce by straining the liquid from the Minted Oranges, and adding the orange juice and honey. Reduce the sauce until it's thick enough to coat a spoon. Adjust the seasoning to taste.

To finish the dish, preheat the oven to 375. Sear the duck breasts in a third skillet. Place the duck breast side up on a roasting pan in the oven for 5–7 minutes. The breasts should be served medium-rare.

For the presentation, slice and arrange an orange on each plate. Slice each duck breast lengthwise into six pieces and arrange them. Pour the sauce over them and serve.

The Best Is Yet to Come

"Clive, I really enjoyed every course at dinner, but I have to tell you, I just loved dessert! To be honest, that's what I looked forward to the most." I wish I had a nickel for every time someone told me something like that. Most of us love desserts. When we're looking at the menu and deciding on our appetizer, salad, soup, and entrée, we sneak a peek at the list of sweets. The very best part of the meal, we're sure, is yet to come.

Tres Leches Cake

In a very similar way, life is like that. The joys and difficulties we encounter each day are test cases and preparations for what is to follow. When things are going well, we can't imagine anything better, but most of us experience hardships of one kind or another throughout our lives. If we resent the difficult situations and sandpaper moments with people, we fail to learn from them. We may fight getting older, but age and wisdom give us the ability to touch others' lives in profound ways.

For many of us, life is different than we anticipated it would be. Yogi Berra famously said, "The future ain't what is used to be." Years ago, we couldn't have anticipated many of the bad things we've experienced, but we wouldn't have guessed that our lives would be filled with such wonderful memories, either. My years in the restaurant and catering business—all of the wonderful and painful experiences—have prepared me for the richest, fullest, and most meaningful part of my life. This book is, in many ways, the culmination of those years of preparation. I've had the pleasure of many wonderful experiences, but now in my own life, I'm convinced, the best is coming.

Desserts may be just fun and flavorful, or they may enable us to linger so we can savor a cherished relationship, or they may be the pinnacle of a celebration of a birthday, an anniversary, or a graduation. Let me share a couple of stories from the restaurant business about desserts and give you several recipes.

When the city was buzzing about something, we tried to capture the spirit of the moment any way we could. In their drive to the playoffs late one summer, the Houston Astros traded for Randy Johnson, one of the top pitchers in baseball. Johnson is a tall, lanky, fierce-looking competitor, and from the moment the trade was announced, the entire city got excited—and Johnson delivered. Every time he pitched, the sold-out Astrodome roared as Johnson struck out batter after batter. His earned run average stayed incredibly low, ending the season at the league's best: 1.28.

RECIPES

Almond Tartlets

Loretta's Cheesecake

Chocolate Cake
(Ganache Frosting)

Tres Leches

Rich Shortbread

A sports writer in the Astros locker room overheard Johnson say that his favorite dessert was cheesecake with strawberry topping. Soon, the writer told me about it. To capitalize on the city's excitement about him, we decided to sell slices of cheesecake for the price of Johnson's ERA, usually between $1.25 and $1.50. Every time he pitched, the number went up or down a little, and we posted his current ERA outside the restaurant every day.

We thought the offer would be popular, but we never imagined that city buses would stop in front of the restaurant so their riders could come in for a delicious piece of cheesecake. Our restaurant became the talk of the town—after, of course, they talked about Randy Johnson and Astros' baseball.

Sam Malone is a popular radio disc jockey in Houston. Years ago, he began coming to our restaurant, and we became friends. Sam enjoyed eating with us so much that he talked about us on air. Soon, guests told us they had heard about our restaurant from Sam.

As a part of our involvement in The Great Tastes of Houston, we often took some of our dishes to the local radio and television stations for the on-air personalities to sample. During one of these visits to Sam's radio station, he told me that he loves chocolate cake. To honor him, we made a special chocolate cake just for him.

One day, we served Sam a piece of chocolate cake, but he said, "Clive, this cake isn't as good as usual. It's too dry." We talked a few minutes, and he told me something I'll never forget: "I don't want to be served something that my eyes say 'I love' but my taste buds say 'I can't stand.'" This experience taught me that too often we focus on the presentation of desserts instead of the taste. After the first bite, the presentation doesn't matter that much, but the flavor produces a lasting memory.

Almond Tartlets

Makes 4 individual tartlets or 1 large tart that serves 6–8

Pastry

8 tablespoons of **butter,** room temperature
2 tablespoons of **sugar**
1 **egg**
½ teaspoon of **baking powder**
1 cup of **all-purpose flour**

Preheat the oven to 400. Use lightly greased, individual, small fruit tart pans or one 10-inch tart pan. Cream the butter and sugar thoroughly, and then add the egg and mix. Add the baking powder and flour, and mix thoroughly. Press small amounts of pastry into the tart pans (approximately ¼-inch thick). Cool them in the refrigerator on a baking sheet.

Filling

6 tablespoons of **butter**
4 tablespoons of **sugar**
1 teaspoon of **vanilla**
1 tablespoon of **milk**
½ cup of **sliced almonds**

Melt the butter, sugar, vanilla, and milk. Add the sliced almonds and stir them into the mixture. Bring the mixture to a simmer and remove it from the heat.

Spoon the mixture into the shells. Place them on a cookie sheet, and bake for 20 minutes. Remove them from the oven and cool them completely on a cake rack.

Loretta's Cheesecake

Loretta Phoenix worked in the kitchen at Charley's for over 20 years. Nobody made this cheesecake like Loretta did.

Makes a 12-inch cake

1 pound of **cream cheese**
1 pint of **sour cream**
1 cup of **sugar**
5 **eggs**
1 teaspoon of **vanilla extract**
1 tablespoon of **lemon juice** and the zest of 1 **lemon**
Optional: ½ cup of **chocolate chips**

Crust

⅓ pound of **graham cracker crumbs**
1 ounce of **all-purpose flour**
2 ounces of **sugar**
2 ounces of **butter,** melted

Preheat the oven to 325.

Cream the cream cheese, then add the ingredients in the order given, one at a time.

Combine all the crust ingredients. Mix well and form it into a layer in the bottom of a springform pan.

Pour the cheesecake mix into the pan. Place the pan in a water bath and bake at 325 for 1 hour. Turn off the oven, prop oven door a little, and let cake sit for 1 hour. (Cover the cake with a moist rag.)

Remove the cake from the oven, and put it into the fridge for about 8 hours.

Serve with choice of topping:

Chocolate sauce
Strawberries, plain or cooked in syrup **(recipe next page)**
Blueberries
Raspberries
A dollop of chutney

Strawberry Sauce

½ cup of **sugar**
1½ tablespoons of **cornstarch**
1 cup of **orange juice**
¼ cup of **Grand Marnier**
6 cups of sliced, hulled **strawberries**

In a 2- to 3-quart saucepan, stir together the sugar, cornstarch, orange juice, and Grand Marnier until it's smooth. Bring it to a boil over medium-high heat, stirring until it's clear and thickened.

Stir in 6 cups of sliced strawberries. Let it cool, and serve on the cheesecake.

Chocolate Cake

Special equipment: use two 10 x 2-inch round cake pans, or it can be made as individual cakes.

Serves 8

3 ounces of fine-quality **semisweet chocolate**
1½ cups of **hot coffee**
3 cups of **sugar**
2½ cups of **all-purpose flour**
1½ cups of **unsweetened cocoa powder**
1 teaspoon of **baking soda**
¾ teaspoon of **baking powder**
1¼ teaspoons of **salt**
3 large **eggs**
¾ cup of **vegetable oil**
1½ cups of **buttermilk**
¾ teaspoon of **vanilla**

Preheat the oven to 325, and grease two pans. Line the bottoms with rounds of waxed paper and grease paper.

Finely chop the chocolate, and in a bowl combine it with hot coffee. Let the mixture stand, stirring occasionally, until the chocolate is melted and the mixture is smooth.

Into a large bowl, sift together the sugar, flour, cocoa powder, baking soda, baking powder, and salt. In another large bowl beat the eggs with an electric mixer until they thickened slightly and are lemon-colored (about 3 minutes with a standing mixer or 5 minutes with a hand-held mixer).

Slowly add oil, buttermilk, vanilla, and the melted chocolate mixture to the eggs, beating until they are combined well. Add the sugar mixture, and beat on medium speed until it is combined well (don't over mix).

Divide the batter between pans, and bake in the middle of the oven until a tester inserted in center comes out clean, 60–70 minutes.

Cool the layers completely in their pans on racks. Run a thin knife around the edges of the pans, and invert the layers onto wire racks. Carefully remove the waxed paper, and cool the layers completely. The cake layers may be made 1 day ahead, kept at room temperature, and wrapped well in plastic wrap.

Ganache Frosting

1 pound of fine-quality **semisweet chocolate,** such as Callebaut

1 cup of **heavy cream**

2 tablespoons of **sugar**

2 tablespoons of **light corn syrup**

½ stick (¼ cup) of **unsalted butter**

Finely chop the chocolate. In a 1½- to 2-quart saucepan, bring the cream, sugar, and corn syrup to a boil over moderately low heat, whisking until the sugar is dissolved. Remove the pan from the heat, and add the chocolate, whisking until the chocolate is melted. Cut the butter into pieces, and add it to the frosting mixture, whisking until it's smooth.

Transfer the frosting to a bowl, and let it cool, stirring occasionally until it's spreadable. (Depending on the kind of chocolate you are using, it may be necessary to chill the frosting until it reaches the desired consistency.)

Spread the frosting between the cake layers and over the top and sides. The cake will stay fresh for up to 3 days if you keep it covered and chilled.

Bring cake to room temperature before serving.

Tres Leches

Serves 12

Cake

9 **eggs,** at room temperature
1½ cups of **sugar**
12 tablespoons of **butter,** softened
2 cups of **all-purpose flour**
1½ teaspoons of **baking powder**
1 cup of **milk**
1 teaspoon of **vanilla extract**
1 teaspoon of **cream of tartar**

Preheat the oven to 350. Separate the egg yolks and whites, keeping the whites at room temperature. In the bowl of an electric mixer, cream the sugar and butter together until it's pale yellow and fluffy. Add the egg yolks and beat it 2–3 minutes on medium-high speed until it's fluffy again. In a separate bowl, combine the flour and baking powder. In a third bowl, mix the milk and vanilla. Alternately add the flour mixture and the milk mixture to the butter mixture (a fourth at a time) until everything is combined, beating after each addition until the mixture is smooth.

Beat the egg whites with cream of tartar until soft peaks form, and using a large spatula, gently but thoroughly fold the egg whites into the flour-and-butter mixture. Grease the bottom of a round 10-inch metal baking pan. Pour in the batter and bake for approximately 25 minutes, until it's golden brown. Allow it to cool. (The cake may also be baked in an 11½ x 17½-inch sheet pan for 20 minutes. This size rises very evenly, which is helpful for inexperienced cooks.)

Three Milks

2 cups of **heavy cream**
1 5-ounce can (⅝ cup) of **evaporated milk**
1 14-ounce can (⅞ cup) of **sweetened condensed milk**

Stir the milks together thoroughly, but don't beat them. And don't refrigerate the canned milks before using them.

Cream Icing

2 cups of **heavy cream**
⅓ cup of **sugar**

Whip the cream and sugar together until it's stiff. When the cake is cool, slice or peel off the thin top crust. Ice the sides first, creating a small lip on top to catch the milk mixture. Pour the milk mixture evenly over the top of the cake. (If necessary, poke holes in cake with a knife or toothpick to facilitate soaking. You'll probably need only ¾ of the mixture). Finish icing the top, and then refrigerate the cake.

(If you're using an 11½ x 17½-inch pan, cut the cake in half to make 2 equal pieces. Soak the first layer, ice the top, and place second layer on top of it. Soak the second layer and ice the top.)

Rich Shortbread

Makes a 10 X 15 baking sheet of shortbread

¾ pound of **butter**
½ cup of **superfine sugar**
3 cups of **all-purpose flour**
A pinch of **salt**
1 cup of **confectioner's sugar**

Preheat the oven to 350.

Cream the butter and sugar, and then add the flour and salt.

Spread the mixture on a baking sheet about ¼-inch thick, and prick it all over with a fork.

Bake it for 20 to 30 minutes until it's a very light golden brown. Sprinkle the shortbread thickly with confectioner's sugar. Cut it into squares while it's hot.

The shortbread can be frozen.

Life's Richest Lessons from the Restaurant Business

Today, life is so hurried that most of us don't even notice the subtle messages and hidden meanings in things that happen to us. In the restaurant business, I tried to stay alert, watching people and situations so that we could serve our guests better. Over time, I tried very hard to develop the habit of looking beyond the obvious to find the meaningful. In the course of our busy lives, we can find wonderful insights every day—we just have to take a minute to look, reflect, and uncover the hidden lessons.

In the last few years, I've spent some time to connect some of the lessons I learned at Charley's to everyday life. When I've shared these thoughts with people, quite often their eyes have lit up and they've said, "You're right. I never thought of that before!" I've already mentioned some of these things in my story, but in this part of the book, I want to explain them a bit more and describe the impact these lessons have had on my cooking and my life.

Sandpaper Moments

Nobody likes conflict or disapproval, but friction occurs from time to time, even in our most valued relationships. In the early years at Charley's, I realized that our very best customers were often those who had previously experienced problems dining with us. On the back of the kitchen door, we posted a sign so that our wait staff would see it every time they came through. It read: "The hardest customer to get is the one you've lost." In our daily meetings with the staff, we talked about our philosophy of service, and we often came back to this principle. If guests had a problem with food or service and we never found out about it to correct it, they were, I'm sure, very reluctant to come back again. And when they're lost, they're often gone for good. But amazingly, some of our most loyal, devoted guests were those who had experienced problems, told us about it, and we bent over backwards to make it right. We experienced friction in the relationship, but our positive and prompt response smoothed things out with them. In the end, our relationship with them was better than ever. I call these "sandpaper moments."

Our restaurant was in the theater district. Unlike any other restaurant I've ever known, our operations were influenced by the shows downtown. On theater nights, almost

> "The hardest customer to get is the one you've lost."

three quarters of our business happened between 6:00 and 8:00 in the evening. We prepared a five-star meal for 140 people, and virtually all of them came in at the same time so they could enjoy their dinners before they had to leave for the theater. They were paying a lot for their meals, and they expected the best. In preparing and presenting 140 memorable meals on time, the pressure was enormous.

One night, a waiter came back to the kitchen and told me that one of our guests was unhappy with his meal. I went out to the table to talk with him. After I introduced myself, he told me plainly, "Clive, your dishes have too many sauces, and the sauces are too heavy."

I tried very hard not to be the least bit defensive, but after all, I'd trained in Europe and had cooked for tens of thousands of people. I could have stared him down and told him I knew far more about cooking that he'd ever imagine, but I didn't. I invited him, "Please tell me what you mean."

He explained that the sauces were covering up the flavor of the key element of the dish, and he thought it would be much better with less and lighter sauces.

I apologized and invited him and his wife to come back at their convenience so I could cook them a special meal according to their tastes. He said he didn't want to do that, but I politely insisted.

Between the evening he complained and the night he came back for dinner a couple of weeks later, I did a lot of thinking about his comments—and I concluded he was right. I changed our entire menu. Instead of putting a tablespoon of sauce on a dish, I put a teaspoon. Instead of using two sauces, I used only one.

When he and his wife returned for dinner, I told him how he had influenced my thinking, and I thanked him. From that day on, they were some of our biggest fans. They came to a few of our vintner dinners, and they told their friends about us.

Sometimes, though, we resist being refined by the friction of sandpaper moments. Years ago when I coached my son's YMCA soccer team, I tried to show off my ball-handling skills to the children (and their parents who were watching), but I slipped and tore a ligament in my knee. For months, I didn't get any treatment. Day after day, I walked on it and endured the pain, but if I turned too sharply, it collapsed and I fell down. One night, the Houston Oilers' team doctor, Robert Fain, Jr., had dinner at the restaurant. As I took some dishes back to the kitchen, my knee gave out and I fell. Dr. Fain heard the commotion and asked what happened. I explained to him about my knee, and he told me to make an appointment to see him. He carefully examined my knee and put me in a brace. Weeks later, however, my knee wasn't any better, so he scheduled surgery. The morning of the surgery, I went to the hospital, was prepped, and lay in a gown on the gurney waiting for the nurse to wheel me into the operating room. As I stared at the ceiling and anticipated the surgeon's knife, all my fears exploded in my mind. When the nurse left the room, I jumped up, grabbed my clothes, and fled from the hospital! This was a sandpaper moment, but I didn't want to be shaped. It was too scary. All of us face moments of friction in various ways: spiritual crossroads, career setbacks, physical pain, or relational conflict. The question is: How will we respond to them? Will we run or stay? Will we resist or change?

Some of the people in my life may not have been exactly what I wanted them to be, but they've been there for a reason: to shape me. All of us can think of people with whom we've experienced friction: husbands, wives, parents, children, business partners, neighbors, friends, and acquaintances of all stripes and forms. I recall an administrative assistant (a role in which I have zero aptitude) who was stubborn, abrasive, and insistent on her own way of doing things. I knew she was right almost all the time, but her attitude rubbed against me. Now, as I look back on that relationship, I can see that my time with her taught me to look beyond her attitude and value her ability to contribute. This was a powerful principle for me to learn.

The lesson of sandpaper moments applies to every relationship in our lives. We can't expect things to go smoothly all the time with everyone. We may want continuous and complete peace, but it simply won't happen. Friction between people, however, doesn't have to destroy the relationship. If we respond by calmly listening, clarifying the problem, reflecting on the solution, and then taking steps to solve the problem, these sandpaper moments can shape our relationships in beautiful ways.

You use steel to sharpen steel, and one friend sharpens another.

Lagniappe

The Cajuns have a wonderful word, lagniappe, which describes a small gift or an extra measure of care for someone. In our restaurant, we wanted people who walked in the door to feel that we were completely devoted to make their dining experience enjoyable and meaningful. We made a point of calling the person by name, and it wasn't as hard as you might think. Guests gave us their names when they called to make reservations, so we made sure our wait staff knew the names of the people they served each night. In the preparation of food, we took extra care to arrange each dish very carefully and add a dash of panache to each plate to make it memorable. When someone got up to go to the restroom, we replaced the napkin with a fresh one. When people celebrated a special occasion with us, like an anniversary or graduation, we steamed the label off their bottle of wine and put it on a copy of the night's menu. As they left, we presented it to them. Each member of the wait staff asked the guests they served for their business cards, and the staff wrote personal thank you notes to those who had been at their tables.

A commitment to do a little extra can enrich and inspire every relationship. Not long ago, I bought theater tickets for my girlfriend and me to attend a Broadway musical that was playing in Houston. On the day we were to attend, something came up, and we couldn't go. I could have given or sold the tickets to almost anyone, but we gave the tickets to a young couple who, we were sure, would really enjoy the show. It was a joy to give them the tickets, and the next day, they told us that this was the first musical they'd ever attended. Their delight made it special for them and for us, too.

Lagniappe can be a part of every day life. To create a moment that's very special, I try to inject it into my catering and in the recipes I give people. For example, I may give someone my recipe for a nice butternut squash soup, but I tell her to add a little cinnamon cream to make it especially good. Shrimp grilled in garlic butter is delicious, but pico de gallo makes it even better. Painter Vincent van Gogh once said, "Great things are not done by impulse, but by a series of small things brought together."

At the restaurant, we never asked our guests, "How did you like your dinner?" Instead, we looked for indications: Where their plates empty? What were their words and facial expressions when they took their first bite? Did they invite their spouse or friends to have a bite? Did they tell us spontaneously how much they enjoyed dinner? When we give people a little extra, we can expect a little extra in their response—in the restaurant or at home.

In every aspect of the restaurant business, we operated by a crystal clear principle: Prior preparation prevents pitifully poor performance, or P^6. When I studied "kitchen French," the first phrase I learned was *mise en place,* prepare in advance. At restaurants, catering, or at home, advanced preparation is absolutely essential if we want to produce something people will enjoy. If you wait until someone orders a dish to wash and cut up the vegetables, get out the spices, and marinate the meat, your guests will be in for a very long evening! We were devoted to excellent preparation so that the chef could focus his or her consummate skills on creating a masterpiece, not rushing to get the veggies chopped and cutting corners to save time. The same principle applies to service. Before the first guests arrived each lunch and dinner, we meticulously prepared each table and rehearsed the specific responsibilities with each of our staff. The first people who came through the doors deserved the same excellence as those who came at peak hours. If we were behind at the beginning, we could never catch up. On those occasions when we got behind, we grumbled to each other, "We're in the weeds."

But let me be very clear: The goal of cooking isn't to produce picture-perfect dishes. You may find perfection in the photography of most cookbooks, but most of these images had to be touched up to hide imperfections. Life, though, isn't like that. In my life and in my cooking, nothing is ever perfect. I want to pursue excellence, but I never want to lose sight of the ultimate objective of doing everything I do to show love to others. An obsession with perfection gets in the way of love. When we fail to prepare well, we get frazzled, but good preparation allows us to keep things in perspective and focus on our top priorities of love and creativity. Famous actor Sir Laurence Olivier once said, "Striving for perfection is the greatest stopper there is. . . . It's your excuse to yourself for not doing anything. Instead, strive for excellence, doing your best." And your best is plenty good enough.

We can offer a taste of lagniappe in a thousand different ways in our homes, and there, we have a distinct advantage: We've watched our family members for years, and we know what they really enjoy. Each person is different. One may feel special when we prepare an elaborate candlelight dinner, another feels loved when we throw a loaf of bread, a hunk of cheese, a couple of apples, and a bottle of wine in a backpack and drive a few miles to a scenic spot for a picnic, and another delights in the presentation of a favorite dessert. You probably already know what each member of your family enjoys, but asking them would start a wonderful conversation. They will appreciate being heard and feeling understood, and you might find out that your previous assumption was wrong (or with teenagers, has changed!).

Many of the recipes in this book include a lagniappe suggestion to make them a little more special, but don't be confined to my suggestions. Try your own—and if they work, tell all your friends.

Tell them to go after God, who piles on all the riches we could ever manage—to do good, to be rich in helping others, to be extravagantly generous. If they do that, they'll build a treasury that will last, gaining life that is truly life.

Oops!

When Hurricane Katrina hit New Orleans in August 2005, over 100,000 people fled to Houston. I was asked to prepare three meals a day for about 7000 that had taken refuge in the George R. Brown Convention Center, and by the third day, I was exhausted. To give me a break, I was given a room in a hotel near the convention center. I fell into bed, but I was so tired I couldn't immediately go to sleep. I turned on the television, and I saw several cooking shows. I didn't grow up watching television, and in Houston, I didn't even have cable at home because I didn't watch very often. All I had were the major networks. As I flipped through the channels in the hotel, one show featured Emeril, and equally well-known chefs hosted other programs. As I watched, I quickly realized something wasn't right. Everything on the 30-minute shows ran perfectly, but that's simply not the way it works in real life, even for the chef of a five-star restaurant. Sometimes, the only tomatoes we can find aren't quite ripe, the sauce needs to be reduced a bit more, or the meat isn't done. No matter how gifted a cook someone might be, we all experience an oops once in a while. One of the biggest challenges to any cook is to respond with grace and creativity when things don't go exactly right. It begins with perspective.

First, don't panic. Accept reality as it is and make the best of it. I believe that most people we serve can accept something that's not perfect as long as we have an explanation for it. If we're defensive and angry, they won't be as gracious. And if we lie and say there's nothing wrong, we'll have a bigger problem than an over-salted soup!

With most oopses, we need a little time to think about a solution—and maybe a phone call to a friend—so we can turn a disaster into something delicious. Sometimes, it takes only a small correction to make a big difference. People may notice, but they'll appreciate our effort to make things work, and even more, they'll be grateful for our poise and grace.

Sometimes, though, the disaster is simply too big to fix. I recall one day when we baked an Italian cream cake, and someone mistakenly thought the salt bin was the sugar bin. It was made with several cups of salt. Not salvageable!

Occasionally, other people unintentionally cause oopses in our lives. One evening, we were asked to cater a New Year's Eve party for some people from South America in a palatial home in River Oaks. We were instructed to serve the hors d' oeuvres at 9:30. We thought they would sit down for dinner at 10:00, but they didn't want dinner until 12:30. I didn't realize their culture dictated the late time for their dinner, and as the clock neared midnight, all the food we had prepared to serve at 10:00 had been sitting for over two hours. When I realized what was happening, I rushed back to the restaurant to prepare a totally new meal to be fresh when they were ready to eat.

Problems—in cooking and every other part of our lives—happen to all of us. If we respond with poise and grace, we provide an incredible role model for our family and friends. Thirteenth century Buddhist monk, Nichiren Daishonin, reflected that difficulties are an inevitable part of life. He wrote, "Never let life's hardships disturb you . . . no one can avoid problems, not even saints or sages."

In our restaurant, we sometimes served dishes that were simply terrible. I wish I could say that I always responded gracefully, but that's not the truth. I'm afraid I have to learn some of the most important lessons the hard way. Over time, though, I discovered that when oopses happened, I needed to do two things: go out of my way to serve the guests and make up for the problem in any way that pleased them (like cooking another meal then or inviting them back for a free meal when they could schedule it), and asking, "What can we

> "Never let life's hardships disturb you . . .
> no one can avoid problems, not even
> saints or sages."
>
> *Nichiren Daishonin*

learn from this mistake?" Blame and anger never accomplish good things, but grace, creativity, and an openness to learn can take us several steps down the road in our cooking skills and with people. And when others make mistakes, the same principles apply. Anger and blame only alienate them and erode the relationship. Offer support and ask, "What can I do to help?" That's a very good response when we (or someone we love) experience an oops.

There's more to come: We continue to shout our praise even when we're hemmed in with troubles, because we know how troubles can develop passionate patience in us, and how that patience in turn forges the tempered steel of virtue, keeping us alert for whatever God will do next.

Before Its Time

A few years ago, a popular wine used the slogan: "We serve no wine before its time." Whether the statement was true for that particular vineyard, I don't know, but it definitely isn't true for the vast majority of us. In our impatience, we serve wine before it reaches its full flavor, and we serve food either too hot or too cold because we won't wait the extra minutes for it to be just right.

Most of the wine we find on the market today is rushed to the store. For the companies that produce it, business principles of productivity rule over culinary principles, and profits are more important than taste. These wines need a bit more (or in some cases, a lot more) time to age, and after we buy them, some of them need to breathe so that the aroma and flavor will be at their peak when we enjoy them. Most Americans serve red wine at "room temperature," but we misunderstand the term. We think this means the temperature of our homes, about 70 degrees Fahrenheit, but we should actually call it "cellar temperature" because red wine is at full flavor at the cooler temperature of wine cellars. And white wines are at their best when they are chilled, but not ice cold.

Each food has an optimum temperature for the best flavor, but too often, we plop everything on a plate and microwave it all together. Some of the foods, like potatoes, need more time to heat in the microwave, and by the time they're right, everything else is nuclear! Far better, serve each course individually instead of all together. This allows people to savor each dish, it makes each one special, and it slows down the rush of eating so that you can enjoy conversation as well as the food. Yes, it takes a few more plates, but most of us have dishwashers, so that's not much of an excuse.

God has designed our sense of taste to be most acute when each food is served at a certain temperature. When it's too hot or too cold, we lose the ability to taste the fullness of the flavor. In addition, different dishes require different temperatures for them to cook properly. If we crank up the heat to get finished quickly, we can ruin a dish. Too often, we take steak off the grill and put it immediately on plates in front of people. If we let it rest in its juices for a few minutes, the richer juiciness and flavor may surprise us. If we overcrowd a saucepan, whether we're boiling potatoes or frying fish, the temperature goes down too much and the dish doesn't cook properly.

Waiting is a lost art in our culture. At the restaurant, we didn't find instant success, but we learned many important lessons as we refined our menu and processes every day. In the restaurant business and in every other aspect of life, we often find more meaning in the process than in the conclusion. For that reason, we need to give more time and attention

to the process of preparation, presentation, and participation in the meal so that we don't wolf down the food to rush to something else. The conclusion of the meal isn't the goal. The focus is the entire process involving creativity and interaction: from shopping to chopping, from adding lagniappe to getting out the best linen, from serving each course individually to a single flower from the garden, from talking about things that really matter with those you love to sitting around after the last bite, from savoring the moment to cleaning up together.

Why are we in such a hurry? I think many of us use external success as a measuring stick, and we aren't content until and unless we reach some lofty, arbitrary goal. To get there, we rush, we push, and we strain to get as much done in as short a time as possible—but our compulsion for speed interferes with the things that truly satisfy: meaningful interaction, creativity, and celebration. Rushing around, then, isn't just a time problem—it's a heart problem. We care too much about the wrong things and too little about the right things.

Why are we so driven? Modern advertising is designed to create a sense of dissatisfaction with our lives, and companies promise that their product or service will make us happy, beautiful, and successful. What we have now, we're convinced, isn't enough. We crave more, so we rush through life trying to fill the hole in our hearts with things that can't possibly fill it. Happiness, as the old saying goes, isn't having what you want; it's wanting what you have. Acceptance, thankfulness, creativity, love, and contentment come from enjoying the process, not from continually running faster and faster for more and more stuff.

Trust God from the bottom of your heart; don't try to figure out everything on your own. Listen for God's voice in everything you do, everywhere you go; he's the one who will keep you on track.

Only the Best

In the restaurant business, we used our equipment every day, and it had to perform. Inferior appliances and utensils break at the most inopportune moments, so we simply couldn't afford to use anything but the best. We may pay a little more, but excellent equipment served us exceptionally well for a long time. The best, though, isn't necessarily the most expensive. "America's Test Kitchen" uses elaborate testing to evaluate a wide range of kitchen equipment, and they've found that quite often the best grill or garlic press or pan or spatula isn't the most expensive one. For anything you want to buy, do a little research to find the best quality available.

We can't make great meals out of inferior ingredients, and we can't turn mediocre raw materials into an excellent dish. When we shop, we need to use common sense to find the very best meats, fish, fruits, vegetables, and dairy products at the market. And I mean "market." I go to markets where I know the food is fresh, and when it's possible, I buy locally grown produce. I love to go to farmer's markets so I can buy from the people who actually grew the beans, tomatoes, and whatever else I'm shopping for.

Some of us don't realize what we're buying at the grocery store. If you don't see fruits and vegetables at a farmer's market, you can be sure the ones at the grocery store are being flown in from a long way away. At certain times of the year, tomatoes are flown in from South America. For them to look red and ripe at the store where we shop, they had to be picked green before they ripened on the vine and reached their peak of flavor. I don't buy tomatoes that were grown halfway around the world, and I only buy flown-in fruits and vegetables that are grown in far off countries if I really need them for a dish. The transportation industry has an amazing ability to ship foods all around the world in a short time, but they still aren't what I would call "fresh." Fruit and vegetables shipped from the Southern Hemisphere in our winter (their summer) may look exactly the same as ours in the summer, but they are days older, not vine ripened. Instead, look for another recipe and buy something

that's fresh. (I want to say, though, that some markets in our area, such as Central Market—my food sanctuary—give attention to quality in their foods that are flown in during the off season. They allow fruits and vegetables to ripen before they are picked, and then they rush them to the store for maximum freshness and flavor.)

Find a store that sells the best meats and fish. Today, many of the meats we buy at the store look fine, but they have very little flavor. If you have to go to a butcher to get a flavorful, tender cut, go there and spend a little more. Fish is notoriously sensitive. Buy only the freshest fish, never ones that have milky eyes or even the slightest fishy odor.

Most supermarkets today have their vegetables and fruits at the entrance of the store. I recommend that you shop for everything else and make any last minute decisions about changing menus and recipes—you may find specials on meat or fish that point your menu in a different direction. Then go to the fresh fruits and vegetables section, select whatever is local and fresh, and go to the check out.

Price, however, isn't necessarily related to quality. Not long ago, I saw a man in a grocery store studying the vast array of bottles of olive oil. I asked, "Can I help you?"

He looked puzzled, so he was glad to have some advice. He asked, "How do I pick an olive oil? The prices range from $4.99 to $19.99. Is there that much difference in quality?"

I answered, "Some come in fancy bottles, and some in plain ones, but when you use them in your dishes, you won't be able to tell the difference between them. I'd pick the $4.99 bottle and spend the extra money on a nicer cut of meat."

Sometimes people asked me if a $5000 bottle of wine was worth the price. In many cases, but not all, the price tag is more about the novelty than the taste. Recently, a blind taste test was performed to see if the price affected people's perceptions of wines. When people tasted the same wine from two glasses, one labeled $5 and the other labeled $45, they consistently claimed the higher priced version tasted better. When they tasted two wines, one an actual $5 bottle and the other a $45 bottle but without labels, they picked the taste of the $5 bottle. The conclusion is this: Pick a wine you enjoy, not one that costs a lot so you can impress your friends.

Unless you are a collector, I don't think any bottle of wine is worth more than $60. Beyond that, pride in the price surpasses taste.

But you would be fed with the finest of wheat; with honey from the rock I would satisfy you.

Don't Lose Your Lunch Money

In our day of so many competing voices, it's easy to be distracted from the things that are really important. When I was a boy in school, my mother gave me lunch money. In the morning recess periods, my friends and I often played marbles. Sometimes I won a little money, but sometimes I lost. On those days, my mother instinctively knew something was wrong when I got home in the afternoon. I told her, "I lost my lunch money." (I didn't tell her that I lost it playing marbles. It was enough just to say it was "lost.")

In every aspect of our lives, it's very easy for us to lose focus, to drift toward those things that capture our attention for the moment and forget the people and values that we truly treasure. Not long ago, I was with a friend at a festival. A beautiful woman walked by, and he shook his head, "I just lost my lunch money because of her."

I was really surprised to hear him make that statement, so I asked, "What do you mean?"

"Oh, it's just a saying I use to mean I could get my eyes on the wrong thing."

I explained, "I've said that my whole life, but I've never heard anybody else say it."

"Losing our lunch money" means drifting off our intended purpose. When we're cooking, we can get our eyes off the importance of the people we serve. We may become obsessed with perfection, or on the other hand, we may just go through the motions with a goal to put barely edible food on a plate two or three times a day. Instead, we need to stay focused on the things that really matter. We can create moments in the kitchen or at the table when those we love take steps to understand each other, comfort those who are hurting, and celebrate successes.

Carving out adequate time for preparation—and having realistic expectations of the entire process of preparing a delicious meal—enables us to stay focused on what's most important.

I would say that the number one reason most people struggle with cooking is that they don't pay enough attention to the preparation phase. They turn on the oven and then start washing and cutting up the food. By then, they're behind schedule, so they hurry and throw it together. Too often, they forget an ingredient or leave out a step, and the dish fails. Or while they're cooking one dish, they're preoccupied with another one, and the first dish burns. Then, they panic and race to the store to get a replacement.

Our usual attempt to solve this problem is to create instant this and microwavable that. In fact, many foods come in a form that require no preparation at all. Whether we fail to adequately prepare when we cook from scratch or we buy prepared foods, either scenario robs us of the joy and creativity of cooking. Attention to preparation enables us to savor the process as much as we enjoy the presentation, the delicious flavor of the meal, and the discussion at dinner.

We need to radically change our concept of cooking and learn from our friends in Europe where cooking is an art, not a race. Like a great painter who spends half his time mixing paints and preparing the canvas, we need to invest time in the things that will produce a wonderful meal for those we love. Yes, some of us are very busy, but at least a few times a week, we need to put ourselves in a slower gear and delight in shopping, washing, cutting, and the preparation of sauces and marinades. Before we turn on the oven or burner, we need to have things ready so we can have enough mental focus to prepare a work of art.

Adequate preparation also reduces stress at the time people arrive for dinner. When we aren't rushed, we feel more at ease and able to focus on the people instead of last-minute preparations. From time to time, I've watched ladies rush around so much that they never got to talk to anyone at dinner or at a party, or they were so exhausted and upset by the stress that they didn't enjoy it. It doesn't have to be that way.

Preparation is important for a good first impression at the front door of a fine restaurant, and it's important for dinner with your family, too. The scale of activities may be different, but it takes only a little extra time and energy to make people feel special. Place a single cut flower from the backyard on the table, take a moment to get out a set of linen napkins instead of using paper, or prepare a special dessert and have it on the table when people walk in. If you take just an extra minute or two, you'll think of many little things you can do to communicate that you treasure the people who sit at your table.

In our culture, most people are afflicted with a terrible disease: hurry sickness. We race from on thing to another. We think we're getting more done, but we're actually paying less attention to creativity and love, the things that make us fully alive. We need to examine our lives and ruthlessly cut out things that infringe on our capacity to experience real life. Devote a little more time to preparation. Try new approaches, present dishes with creativity and zest, and experience the joy of cooking and dining as works of art.

The principles of preparation apply to every area of our lives. When we slow down, we have time for a moment of reflection so that we see people and events in perspective instead of just reacting to them. With a little insight, we can see that the past has prepared us for the present. Some of the things that shaped our lives seemed like interference or detours at the time (like my tour of duty in the army). Too often, we use past hurts and discouragements as excuses to avoid reflecting, so we hurry more to try to fill up the hole in our hearts.

Devoting enough time to preparation enables us to give attention to detail, and good preparation can become a habit instead of an intrusion. In a fine restaurant, guests notice the quality of the linen in tablecloths and napkins, the arrangement of the silver, the placement of salt and pepper, the freshness of flowers, the starch in the wait staff's uniforms, and every aspect of presentation of the food and service. Of course, not every guest notices everything, but they all notice something. I learned the importance of outstanding service from Victor Broceaux in Miami, and his example and standards shaped my career and my life. Author and teacher Marva Collins wrote, "Excellence is not an act but a habit. The things you do the most are the things you do the best."

"Excellence is not an act but a habit. The things you do the most are the things you do the best."

Marva Collins

If we take a moment, we can think of small choices that say a lot to our friends and family. Buying fresh spices for a nice meal adds to the flavor of a dish. Putting a sprig of parsley on a plate says, "I care about you." A colorful side-dish adds interest because "people eat with their eyes." Instead of drinking sodas from cans, we can put ice in glasses on the table.

A lovely presentation, though, isn't the ultimate goal of a meal. When people take their first bite, they've altered the way the food looks on the plate. At that point, the most important thing is the taste: Do they relish taking their second bite? Don't become fixed on the way a dish looks and neglect the flavor. And to broaden the principle to the rest of our lives, we shouldn't spend inordinate time and energy on our own appearance and neglect the condition of our hearts.

Attention to detail honors the people we love, and it provides a good example for our children. If they only see us racing through life and eating on the run, the image that speed is more important than people becomes imprinted on their minds. Don't let bad habits continue. If you need to spend a bit more time to honor them at meal times, spend it. If you have to change your schedule, change it. Some things are more important than others. Many urgent things aren't important, but sadly, most really important things don't seem urgent, so we neglect them. Determine what's really important, and set your schedule to fit your priorities.

Involve your family in preparation and presentation, and let them contribute to your attention to detail. Make it a delight, not a chore. If they see your creativity and joy in cooking, they'll be much more likely to participate gladly—and they'll model that value to their own children one day. Not long ago, my son Ian asked me to help him prepare dinner for his girlfriend's birthday. We went to the market to buy tenderloin and other things for dinner, and we bought ingredients for him to bake a cake for her. We prepared dinner together and baked the cake. During the process, he set the table to perfection. He made every part of the dinner truly special. To be honest, I don't remember ever "training" him about doing things with creativity and excellence, but he must have been watching. To him, it wasn't a chore—not in the least. He was thrilled to honor someone he cares for.

We are creatures of habit. A lifestyle of rushing through life, cutting corners, being too tired to connect with people, and ending up frustrated and empty has become a habit for too many of us. But habits can change. They just take a little extra effort at the beginning to overcome inertia. For a week, make a concerted point to carve out a few extra minutes to give attention to detail so that you can honor the people you love. In only a week, you will be on your way to a new habit in cooking—and perhaps, a new lifestyle.

I don't think we can express our love if we're competing with the television. We need to turn it off. You and your family may need time to relearn how to connect with each other and enjoy conversation, but after a few awkward dinners of adjustment, you'll wonder why it took you so long to make the change. When people eat together in a relaxed, loving environment, they are a little more vulnerable, a little more open, and a little more patient with one another.

Most of us put the entire meal on a single plate, and we eat like the goal is to consume enough calories to survive. But meals are meant to build relationships with those we love. Instead of wolfing down our food, we can stage the meal as a process that mirrors the ebb and flow of life. We begin with an appetizer that whets our appetites, we have a salad or soup to get us ready for the main course, and then we savor the rich flavor of the meat and vegetables. At the end, we enjoy the dessert we've looked forward to all along, like heaven that we long to experience someday.

In the rest of our lives, too, we can easily get distracted. Instead of pursuing excellence in our marriages and relationships with children and friends, we can drift into complacency. After a while, some behaviors that had seemed unthinkable become thinkable, and soon, the improbable becomes a destructive course of action. An initial mental distraction gradually escalates into a full-blown catastrophe. Whether distractions numb us or excite us, they take us away from the things that really matter.

After about two years at Charley's, I became terribly frustrated with the chef, but the president of the company insisted that we keep her. I reached a point that I couldn't stand it any longer, so I decided to look for another job. (Talk about avoiding sandpaper!) Another restaurant offered me a position, and I accepted it. When I resigned from Charley's, the president took me out to lunch and persuaded me to stay. Over the next several years, the other restaurant changed hands three times. I realized that if I had accepted that position, I probably would have had a rough time during all the transitions and would have lost my job at some point, and worse, I would have missed all the experiences we had at Charley's. When I looked for another job, I temporarily lost my focus, and I almost suffered severely from it.

On the other extreme, it's certainly possible to become too intently focused on something or someone. I know; I did it. For years, running the restaurant was an obsession to me. It was my identity and the source of my energy. I thought about it from the time I got up each morning until my last waking moments. And if I could put my dreams on a DVD, they'd probably have been about the restaurant, too. When I got married, my heart was directed to my wife and my son, but the pain of the divorce spoke loudly (and deceptively) to me that I couldn't trust anyone and I shouldn't give my heart to anyone ever again. What a disastrous conclusion.

Without the anchor of a loving relationship, I tried to find meaning in my work, and my perfectionist tendencies ran unchecked. I fully believe that attention to detail is important, but it shouldn't be a god. Perfectionism, though, wasn't my only foolish path. In our drive to keep the restaurant and grow our business, we borrowed money. The Bible says that the borrower becomes a slave to the lender, and that's exactly what happened. The bank and investors owned not only the note to the restaurant; they owned me, too. Under the pressure of the debt, everything I thought, said, and did was designed to make enough people happy so they'd come to our restaurant so we could pay the next note payment. I loved cooking and serving, but far too often, the joy I could have experienced was clouded—or crushed—by the specter of debt.

Change occurs for some of us only when we're truly desperate. When Charley's burned, I was devastated. My reason for existence went up in smoke and crumbled into ashes. I was depressed, and I had to look inside to see what was important to me. Ironically, the disaster was the beginning point for wisdom and hope. I realized that the restaurant controlled me instead of me controlling it.

I wish people experienced change more easily, but most of us don't. We hang on to obsessive desires and destructive behaviors until the pain of clinging to them is surpassed by our desperate desire for life to be different. At various times and in various ways, all of us tend to put the wrong thing in the center of our lives. The question I ask others and myself is this: "What have you been thinking about all day today?" The answer to that question says a lot about what or who is controlling our lives. Without intending for it to happen, it's easy to drift away from the things we know are most important. Soon, the priorities of our relationships with God and people can pale in the glaring light of the promises of success, pleasure, and approval.

When we don't know what to do, we shouldn't panic and make a snap decision. We should slow down, think carefully, talk to wise friends, and wait for a good answer to surface. Noah had to wait a long time during a storm and on the sea until he touched land. Helen Keller wrote, "When one door of happiness closes, another opens; but often we look so long at the closed door that we do not see the one which has been opened for us."

In my life, calamity was the beginning of change. I wish I could have learned some other way, but I'm very grateful to God that he used something to get my attention. Today, I still have the tendency to drift from the things that are truly valuable to those that promise what they can't deliver, but I'm at least aware of the struggle, so I can fight each day.

The restaurant business was, in many ways, wonderful for me. It fit my passions, skills, and personality, but until calamity and God rearranged my priorities, I was a slave to it. Today, I try to keep cooking where it belongs: as a gift to enjoy and a skill to impart to people who want to use food as a way to honor those they love.

All of us are prone to "lose our lunch money," and none of us is immune from the danger of drift. We are wise to recognize it and fill our lives with meaning. To do that, we need to slow down, savor the process as much or more than the end result, and delight in people and God each step along the way.

So let's keep focused on that goal, those of us who want everything God has for us. If any of you have something else in mind, something less than total commitment, God will clear your blurred vision—you'll see it yet! Now that we're on the right track, let's stay on it.

Let Me Suggest
... Some Tips for
Every Cook

Over the years, I've learned a lot of things that can help people excel a bit more at every aspect of cooking, from creative menus to shopping to preparation to cooking to presentations to handling leftovers. Let me give you a few suggestions. (You may recognize a few of them from other parts of the book.) As you read them, put a mark next to the ones you want to try. Then, in a few months come back and read the list again. There may be another tip or two you want to try.

231

Equipment

* For *kitchen equipment*, buy only what you
  need, not sets. I've found that most people
  use only a few items in sets of pots, pans,
  bowls, and knives, and the others clutter up
  the kitchen. I recommend:
  * 1 large, heavy iron pot, about 8 quarts (I recommend La Creuset, which will last
    a lifetime.)
  * 1 4-quart pot (I recommend All-Clad and Calphalon.)
  * 1 small, 2-quart pot for small quantities (All-Clad and Calphalon)
  * 1 non-stick skillet (Buy an inexpensive one and replace it when it wears out.)
  * 1 heavy-duty frying pan with deep sides (All-Clad and Calphalon)
  * Buy the best knives you can afford, except for the bread knife. You can buy a less
    expensive brand for that one. I recommend:
    * a cook's knife
    * a paring knife
    * a boning/filet knife
    * a bread knife

* Sharpen your *knives* every time you use them. Keep a sharpener nearby so you don't
  have to look for it each time you use a knife. If your knives become dull, it's very
  difficult to return them to their original sharpness. If they become too dull, find a
  professional sharpener (sometimes found at fine grocery stores) to restore them.

* Find a heavy wire or plastic container to keep all your *cooking liquids*—wines,
  sauces, oils, etc. When you cook, put the container on the counter where everything is easily accessible. Then, when you've finished, put the container back in the
  pantry. You'll be surprised how much time this saves from searching for each bottle
  every time you cook.

Ingredients

* Throw out every grain of *iodized salt* in your house, and use sea salt, which has much better flavor and less sodium. Try sea salt from different parts of the world; each one has a distinct flavor.

* *Salt* a little before cooking, and salt when the dish is done to season it perfectly to taste.

* Create a 4 to 1 mixture of *sea salt and white pepper* as your standard seasoning. Have it next to the stove at all times.

* Get rid of every recipe in your home that calls for *green bell peppers*. They are the worst vegetable in the world and have the most peculiar taste of any food. They don't add anything good to any recipe. Use red or yellow varieties instead.

* I may have to duck when I say this because I live in Texas, but I'd say the same thing about *jalapeño peppers*. They have a very odd taste. Instead, use serrano or poblano peppers, which have a much better flavor and balance.

* The *dressing* for a salad can make or break a meal. Many of dressings bought at the store, though, aren't very good. Instead, make your own. They'll be fresher and have far better flavor for a fraction of the cost.

* Buy *fresh herbs* for each meal or each week's menu. Store the fresh herbs in bags, and use clothespins or clips to seal them. Don't let the bags press down on each other. Hang the bags up so the herbs stay as fresh as possible

* Buy *fresh spices* for each meal or each week's menu, too. Don't buy large bottles of spices because they lose their flavor by the time you finish using all of them. Buy only what you need for the next few days. You'll be surprised at how much flavor fresh spices add to your dishes.

* There's no such thing as a *"cooking wine."* If you wouldn't drink it, why would you cook with it?

* Don't buy *fish* at large supermarkets because their product rotation usually is too slow. Find a shop that specializes in the best meats and fish, one that is very busy and rotates food very quickly. Use your senses when shopping for fish. Does it look fresh and vibrant, or does it look pale? Ask to smell a fish or a fillet. If it smells fishy, don't buy it. Fresh fish should smell like the water it came from, not like an old, dead fish carcass.

* 1 tablespoon of *fresh herbs* equals about 1 teaspoon of dried herbs.

* The tailpiece of the tenderloin, the *Filet mignon,* is delicious for sandwiches, stroganoff, or stir fry.

* *Garlic* is an exceptional food, adding flavor to many dishes. Here are some interesting things about it:

  • The scientific name for garlic is "allium sativum." It's related to the lily and the onion. Though garlic has a flavor that slightly resembles an onion's, chopped or minced garlic doesn't bring tears to our eyes.

  • Over time, garlic softens and begins to sprout, which turns the garlic bitter. To keep it fresh, store it in a dark, cool place. Don't refrigerate or freeze garlic because exposure to cold causes it to lose its taste.

  • To peel a clove of garlic, place it on a cutting board, and put the flat of the blade of the knife against it. Press down on the other side of the blade with the heel of your hand, flattening the garlic slightly. The skin will come right off.

- The strong flavor and odor of garlic come from sulfur compounds in the cells. Breaking more cells creates a stronger flavor. For the mildest flavor, use a whole or slightly crushed clove. For a stronger flavor, slice or chop the garlic, and for the strongest flavor, mash the garlic into a paste. Cooking garlic reduces the strong flavor and changes it in different ways, depending on how it's cooked.

- If you're using garlic in a sauce, it can be sweated or sautéed. To sweat the garlic, first finely chop it, and then add it to a cold pan with some oil. Gently heat it, causing the oil to become infused with the garlic flavor.

- To sauté garlic, heat the oil in the pan first, and then add the chopped garlic, stirring frequently. Be careful not to let the garlic burn and become bitter.

- Roasting garlic softens the flavor and makes it perfect for mixing with cream cheese to spread on toast (or spread on the toast by itself). To roast it, remove the papery outer skin from a whole head of garlic. Place it on a piece of aluminum foil, and drizzle with some olive oil. Loosely wrap the garlic in the foil, and place it in a 350-degree oven for 1 hour. Remove the garlic and let it cool. When it's cool enough to handle, separate the cloves of garlic, and squeeze each one. The flesh should pop right out. Roasted garlic mixes well with cheese or potatoes, or you can use it on its own.

- Don't be afraid to use garlic in your cooking. It's flavorful, healthful, and of course, it will keep those pesky vampires away!

Methods

* Keep your *cookbooks* in the living room or next to your bed so you can read them at a leisurely pace and think about each recipe.

* As much as possible, prepare recipes *from memory* . When you become so familiar with preparing a dish so that you know the ingredients, the amounts, and the process, leave the cookbook on the shelf. This way, you'll become more confident, and you'll probably be more creative in your cooking.

* Very few people need to heed President Truman's advice: "If you can't stand the heat, get out of the kitchen." Almost *anybody* can learn to cook, and even become a good cook. My mother did it, and so can you.

* Stick with what you do best. *Experiment* with new recipes when you cook for your family, not when you host big dinner parties or important guests.

* Make *lagniappe* a regular part of your preparation. Be creative; try new things. For example, instead of using the classic recipe for bruschetta, add a twist. Put a little olive oil on the bread and toast it, then, when it comes from the oven, rub it with a garlic clove. To give it a bit of flair, spread a little cream cheese or goat cheese on it before putting on the other ingredients

* Learn from the *best chef* you know. Most of us have an aunt, grandmother, father, close friend, or someone else who is a great cook. Spend time with that person, and soak up all the insights and skills you can. Don't be afraid to ask for recipes, and if they say, "Oh, I've cooked this all my life. I don't have it written down," ask them to tell you what they do and write it down for yourself.

* Learn *how long* foods last, and date your leftovers. From time to time, all of us have found food in the refrigerator that looks good, but we can't remember when we cooked it. When you put leftovers in the refrigerator, put a piece of tape with the date on it so you'll know how long it's been in there.

* If you wonder if *leftovers* are too old to eat, throw them out. Don't settle for them looking good. A good sniff test is more reliable, but some of us can't rely on that either. Don't take chances with food poisoning.

* Let food cool to *room temperature* before you wrap it up and put it in the refrigerator. If you cover it when it's hot, the steam has nowhere to go, and bacteria will form.

* Reduce your leftovers' contact with air by wrapping them with *plastic wrap* before you close the lids on the containers. Some people even put aluminum foil over the plastic wrap to prevent odors from escaping and entering. Most people have to throw food out much too soon because they don't wrap and chill it correctly.

* At the finest restaurants, people order four to seven courses for dinner, so the *portions* are appropriately proportioned. In most restaurants today, however, servings sizes have become enormous. When I go out to eat with someone, we almost always share the entrée. We may each get an appetizer, or we may share it; we may each get a salad, or we may share that too. And we almost always share dessert. Ordering this way not only saves money; it brings two people together because they talk about what they like, agree on each dish, and enjoy each course together.

* If you want to determine the *quality* of a restaurant before dining, go into the restroom and look at their attention to detail there. One look will tell you all you need to know.

* To keep *potatoes* from budding, put an apple in the bag with them.

* To make perfectly formed *pancakes*, use a meat baster to squeeze batter onto the hot griddle.

* When you boil *corn on the cob*, add a pinch of sugar to the water to bring out the natural sweetness of the corn.

* Wrap *celery* in aluminum foil and put it in the refrigerator, and it'll stay fresh for a long time.

* If your *food is ready* but your guests aren't ready to sit down, put it in the oven on 170 degrees.

* To make *clarified butter*, melt the butter, pour cracked wheat on it, and strain through a sieve to remove the sediment and protein.

* Put a moist paper towel under your *cutting board* to keep it from slipping.

* When you cook, wear *comfortable clothes*, ones that you don't mind spilling sauce on. You might want to buy a $20 chef's short-sleeve jacket to slip over your clothes or to wear by itself.

* If a recipe calls for two *large eggs*, you can substitute three smaller ones.

* Some recipes call for ingredients to be *caramelized*, which allows the natural sugars to begin to take color. Butter or oil helps this process in vegetables.

* To make an *egg wash*, mix 1 egg with 1–2 tablespoons of milk or water. For a darker crust, use less liquid.

Preparation

In the restaurant business or at home, preparation makes the difference between enjoyment and chaos, delicious dishes and dreadful messes. When we watch cooking shows on television, we don't get an accurate picture of the process. It looks like the herbs chopped themselves and climbed into a cup, the egg was already

cracked into a ramekin, and one ramekin magically contains grated cheddar cheese and another has perfectly measured and sifted 4 ounces of flour. All this preparation makes it possible for the chef to focus on creativity and conversation instead of rushing to get each ingredient prepared while he's cooking. Remember: Prior preparation prevents pitifully poor performance. Here are some suggestions for you:

* *Prepare your work area.*

When I hold cooking demonstrations in homes, the hosts often warn me that the kitchen won't be big enough. They shouldn't worry. To make delicious meals for your family, you don't need a state-of-the art gourmet kitchen with a huge island and miles of counter space. All you need is an oven, a stove, a sink, and about six square feet of counter space. If the recipe requires prepping meats or vegetables, you may want to set aside a little counter space next to your sink for the cutting board so clean up will be easier. Before you begin, take a moment to look at your kitchen countertop and remove the homework, bills, appliances you aren't going to use, Barbie dolls, and car keys. Don't start preparing the meal until you have enough space to work comfortably.

* *Read the recipe completely.*

The only surprise you want to experience in your cooking is how delightful your dishes turn out. You can eliminate a host of unwelcome surprises simply by reading the recipes very carefully before you begin to prepare and cook. It might be helpful to visualize each step to be sure you have the appliances and products you'll need.

* *Gather your tools.*

Before you begin, put all of the tools you'll be using on the countertop. Delicate sauces can ruin while you root around in the drawer for the right whisk! Recently, I wanted to make a butternut squash soup. I got well into the preparation when I realized I had loaned the immersion blender to a friend. If I'd checked everything in advance, I wouldn't have gotten stuck in the middle of the cooking process. And gather all of your ingredients. Place your meats, vegetables, spices, canned goods, and everything else in a designated area on the counter. The recipe may call for necessary preparation before cooking begins, such as cubing meats, chopping vegetables, and lightly beating eggs, and you'll have everything you need. One day, you may become a famous cook with your own sous chef, but for now, you have to prepare everything yourself—or better, with the help of your family. Your attention to detail in preparation will be a wonderful example for them to follow.

* *Mise en place.*

This French term means having all your tools ready and ingredients prepared and pre-measured in small dishes, ready to add at the prescribed time. This technique, used by chefs to make preparing meals easier, will help you to become a better cook, too. Here are a few examples of mise en place: separating the yolks and whites of eggs, chopping and measuring a cup of onions, and measuring all the spices you'll need. You don't have to buy special bowls. All you need are a few small containers—coffee cups, custard cups, and even cereal bowls will do.

Grilling

Some people are masters of grilling because they've learned a few important lessons about grilling meats and fish. Let me give you a few suggestions:

* Before each use, *clean and lightly oil* your grill. Be sure to clean the collecting pans and drains, too.

* If you have a *gas grill* with multiple burners, use one at high temperature, one on medium, and one on low.

* Depending on the type of meat, *start on high* or medium and finish on low heat.

* Never use a *fork* to turn meat. Use tongs to avoid piercing the meat and losing flavorful juices.

* Determine how you want your meat cooked, and use a *meat thermometer:* rare: 130, medium rare: 140, medium: 150, and well done: 160. (Remember that meat continues to cook after it's taken off the grill.)

* All meat should be taken out of the refrigerator, covered, and allowed to come to *room temperature* for up to 1 hour before grilling.

* The *tools* you'll need for grilling are:
  - Long-handled tongs
  - A long-handled spatula for fish
  - A food mop or brush to baste meats or fish with marinade
  - A wire brush for cleaning the grill
  - A water spray bottle to keep flames down

* To grill *fish or shellfish,* try these methods:
  - A hinged wire grill basket is best for cooking whole fish such as snapper, trout or salmon. It also works well for fillets of tender fish such as perch, snapper, catfish or flounder.

  - Skewer small shellfish such as shrimp or scallops on metal or water-soaked wooden skewers or cook them in a grill basket.

  - If you are going to save the marinade and use it as an extra sauce on the cooked fish or seafood, the marinade liquid must be boiled by itself for at least three minutes to cook out any bacteria that may have multiplied when the fish was soaking.

  - To grill shellfish in the shell, such as oysters, mussels, and clams, place them directly on the hottest part of the grill. They're done when the shell opens. Discard those that don't open after about five minutes..

Wine

* To keep *leftover wines* fresh to use in cooking, pour them into ice trays and freeze them and then store the bag of cubes in the freezer. If you intend to use the wine in your cooking in the next week or two, put a cork in the bottle and keep it in the refrigerator.

* Serving wine at the *correct temperature* is the single most important factor to enjoy it. Serve red wine at cellar temperature, about 62 degrees Fahrenheit, not "room temperature." Put the bottle in the refrigerator for 20 minutes. And serve white wine chilled, but not ice cold—cold enough to be pleasant without masking the flavors. Forty-five minutes in the refrigerator should be sufficient.

* Wine can't *breathe* properly through the narrow neck of a bottle. Pour it into a carafe or a decanter. White wines need 15–20 minutes; reds need about 30 minutes.

Menu Planning

* Don't serve the *same meat or poultry* twice in a row, even if they are prepared differently.

* Make sure you have a *variety of colors* in your menu.

* Vary *garnishes* from item to item.

* Use a variety of *cooking methods* in the same meal: grill, poach, bake, and sauté.

* Vary *textures*, such as crunchy and mousse. For example, ice cream in a cone works well. Don't have too many creamy dishes in one meal.

* Consider the *time of year*, and use fruits and vegetables that are in season.

* Be aware of the *weather* and plan your menu so that you serve lighter items in hot weather.

* Rich dishes need a *tart, savory accompaniment*, such as a sauce or relish.

* Avoid having a menu with all *cold items*.

* *Light desserts* should follow heavy menus. Serve chocolate sweets when you serve light meats and serve tart desserts after serving fish.

* Preparation and *timing* are crucial. Prepare as much as possible in advance. Try to have at least two dishes (such as soup, salad, sauces, and accompaniments) fully prepared in advance so you can devote your full attention to a few other dishes.

* Don't serve *massive quantities* of food. Remember: Less is more, and quality is the focus.

* Keep a *list of menus* you serve to your guests so that you don't repeat the same dish for the same people.

* For *formal dinners*, offer four or five courses, including soup, salad, fish, meat, and dessert.

Your Fridge: The Home for Your Food

Your refrigerator is the living room, den, and bedroom for much of the food you prepare for those you love. For your fridge to serve you best...

* Make it shine!

Use some elbow grease and give the shelves, drawers, and crisper a good cleaning. A mixture of white vinegar and bicarbonate of soda is the best cleaner for the fridge.

* Group things together

Group similar foods together. For example, place drinks on one shelf, small snacks in a drawer, and fruits/veggies/salad products in the crisper so you don't have to search for the food you need at that moment.

* Group by similar heights

Pay attention to the heights of your jars and bottles. It's easier to find things if you put large and tall jars toward the back of the refrigerator and smaller ones in the front. You'll never see that container of yogurt if it's trapped behind a family-sized jar of spaghetti sauce!

* Give them a home

Have you ever seen a bag of fresh herbs flattened by a bag of sliced smoked turkey? Or you may find a bag of shredded cheese three weeks after you needed it in a recipe because it was covered by a bag of apples. Instead of having a flat package of Swiss cheese teetering atop a jar, or the shredded mozzarella flattened by package of steaks, put all the cheeses together in one plastic container. This is a perfect solution if you have small, similar items floating around your fridge. If you have young children, you can create a container for each child and fill it with healthy snacks, punch boxes, and a loving note. This keeps little fingers from rummaging through the shelves, and you can control what goes into their snack boxes.

* Give them a quality home

To ensure that your containers work for you and not against you, spend a few extra pennies on quality containers. On quality products, the lids are less likely to get stuck or fly off, saving you from having to clean the floor or remove stains from your shirt because your container failed to do its job. Choose transparent or translucent containers so you can see exactly what's inside—no surprises!

* Give them the same home

Keep your refrigerator organized by always putting foods and drinks to the homes you've designated for them. Throwing your groceries in the fridge when you come back from the store may save you a few seconds, but it will cost you valuable minutes at meal planning and preparation time.

* Make it a habit

In order to keep your fridge clean and uncluttered, purge it as part of your weekly housecleaning routine. Regularly dispose of smelly substances, rotting vegetables, old leftovers, and other items that have overstayed their welcome. A few minutes each week will keep your fridge in tip-top shape. With determination, patience, and good habits, your refrigerator can become an organized and functional part of your home.

Index of Recipes

Cooking Demonstrations

Clive conducts cooking demonstrations for intimate dinner parties or large events. He combines an entertaining style, delicious food, and a lesson or two about life. Large organizations, like church groups, use Clive to connect with people in their communities. For more information about scheduling an event with Clive, go to CookingwithClive.com.

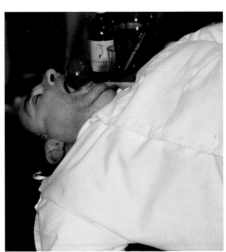

CookingwithClive.com

CookingwithClive.com is a fun, informative, interactive site where you can find delicious new recipes, be inspired by (and laugh a little at) Clive's blog, discover the topics Clive speaks on, schedule an event, and explore all the resources available for you.

Acknowledgements

From my first conversations with the publisher about this book, we realized this is more than a cookbook — it's about creating extraordinary meals that build relationships and produce wonderful memories. As I think about all the people who have been instrumental in shaping my life and helping me with this book, my heart is truly filled with gratitude.

* In my family, I want to thank:

    My son Ian, the light of my life and the joy of my heart.

    My mother Maureen, for always keeping me focused on what's most important in life, and who proofed all the recipes and gave me wonderful feedback.

    My brother Tony, for believing in me.

    My sister Patricia, for her encouragement, and for her husband Mark, who delights in eating as much as anybody I've ever known.

    Jacob and Michael, for the fun of being around them.

    My family in Israel—Louis, Lorna, Bev, Suzanne, Nir, Boz, and the children—for the empty bottle moments I enjoyed with them.

* To those who participated with me at Charley's 517, Crème de la Crème, and True Concessions, I want to thank:

    Bill Sharman, my partner and the founder of Charley's.

    Terry and Mary Murphree, who have been wonderful supporters over the years.

    Dean, Brando, Kevin, Sam, Alvino, Tarek, and Loretta, who were simply the best in the business.

    Dr. Robert Fain, Jr., the ultimate creator of empty bottle moments.

    All the guests that passed through our doors and dined in tents, and who allowed me to be part of their memories.

✳ At our church, I want to thank:

> Dr. Edwin Young, who introduced me to the source of life.

> Lisa Milne, whose friendship and support mean so much to me.

> Dr. James DeLoach, for his undying encouragement, consistent words of truth, and positive influence on me.

> Dr. Gary Moore, who first conceived "Cooking with Clive" events and profoundly shaped the quality of everything I do.

> Craig Reynolds, for his support and guidance.

> The staff and family of Second Baptist Church, for their hearts, their love, and their enthusiasm in following God.

✳ Many friends have encouraged me to write this book, and I want to thank:

> Pat Frazier, for his persistent affirmation and friendship.

> Mark and Lisa Ammerman, for their faith in me.

> David and Valerie Hanson, who shared many wonderful empty bottle moments with me in their home at Thanksgiving and Christmas.

> Tim Mavergeorge, who connected me with his friend Pat Springle, my publisher.

✳ Some very creative people have contributed to this book, and I want to thank:

> Scott Brignac, for his outstanding work on the cover and the web site.

> Nino, at Flowers by Nino, for the beautiful arrangements at our photo shoots.

> Danielle, at The Perfect Face, for making me look younger than I am.

> Anne McLaughlin, for her incredible design of the interior of the book.

> Michelle Gooding, for her outstanding job proofing the manuscript.

> Cody Bess and David Collins, for their wonderful photographs.

> Annel Ochoa, for all her help in producing the food for the photographs.

Michael and Kasandra Windstone, Martha and Richard Owens, and Kathy and
Craig Johnson, for allowing the photo shoots in their lovely homes.

Pat Springle, who shepherded the process of writing and publishing the book.

And all those friends who helped in many different ways and said I didn't need to
mention their names.

Thanks to all of you!

Photo Credits

David Collins
Photo of Clive on back flap of dust jacket, photos of Clive's family and herbs on front end-sheet, both photos on back endsheet, plus photos on pages 43, 54, 55, 58, 59, 62, 63, 69, 79, 80, 81, 84, 91, 94, 99, 101, 102, 106, 107, 108, 109, 110, 112, 114, 116, 117, 120, 121, 122, 130, 134, 135, 138, 146, 149, 151, 152, 153, 154, 155, 162, 164, 170, 177, 186, 189, 191, 193, 195, 197, 200, 204, 207, 208, 211, 214, 215, 216, 218, 220, 224, 226, 229, 232, 238, 243, 245, and 250.

Cody Bess
Front and back cover photography, photo of bottles on front endsheet, photos on edge of all pages, plus photos on pages 12, 46, 65, 68, 72, 76, 77, 78, 85, 86, 93, 100, 131, 141, 142, 143, 144, 156, 159, 161, 163, 182, 196, 198, 230, 233, and 234.

True Color Studios
Photo on page 127.

Don Kellam
Photo on page 45.

istockphoto.com
Photos on pages 61, 71, 73, 75, 137, 150, 168, 173, 176, 179, 181, 183, 212, and 219.

city-data.com
Photo on page 67.

PhotoDisc
Photos on pages 169 and 174.

To Order More Copies of the Book

Go to *www.CookingwithClive.com*

Many people enjoy giving books like this to their friends for Christmas, birthdays, and other special occasions, so discounts are available for large orders.

Empty Bottle Journal

Think back over your life. What are some of the most meaningful and memorable times you've had with friends and family? Note them, and describe what was most meaningful to you about each one.

As you have more empty bottle moments, put the date, place, and people involved. Describe what made it a memorable occasion. From time to time, read over your list to remember how rich your life has become.